CryENGINE Game Programming with C++, C#, and Lua

Get to grips with the essential tools for developing games with the awesome and powerful CryENGINE

Filip Lundgren

Ruan Pearce-Authers

BIRMINGHAM - MUMBAI

CryENGINE Game Programming with C++, C#, and Lua

First published: November 2013

Production Reference: 1151113

Published by Packt Publishing Ltd.

Livery Place
35 Livery Street
Birmingham B3 2PB, UK.

ISBN 978-1-84969-590-9

www.packtpub.com

Cover Image by Carl-Filip Lundgren (filip@poppermost.se)

Credits

Authors
Filip Lundgren
Ruan Pearce-Authers

Reviewers
Terry Evans
Chris Parthemos
Hendrik Polczynski
Ross Rothenstine

Acquisition Editor
Sam Wood

Lead Technical Editor
Arun Nadar

Technical Editors
Anusri Ramchandran
Rohit Kumar Singh

Project Coordinator
Kranti Berde

Proofreaders
Dirk Manuel
Lindsey Thomas

Indexer
Rekha Nair

Graphics
Ronak Dhruv
Abhinash Sahu

Production Coordinators
Aditi Gajjar
Adonia Jones

Cover Work
Adonia Jones

About the Authors

Filip Lundgren is a Technical Director at Poppermost Production AB where he works on SNOW, the first free-to-play open-world skiing title. Filip has been working with CryENGINE since 2007 with the release of Crysis 1 SDK, and has developed community tools such as CryMono and the CryENGINE toolbox.

> Writing the book was a great experience and has involved the help of many CryENGINE community members. Many thanks to the CryDev community and our reviewers for valuable input that helped shape the book to what it is now.

Ruan Pearce-Authers is a game programmer currently working for Crytek GmbH. In 2009, he began managing Crytek's development community, and providing technical support for CryENGINE users. Prior to this, he was active in the Crysis modding community himself, and followed this up by producing sample projects and additional tools for the Free SDK. He co-developed the CryMono engine extension to bring support for .NET to the CryENGINE, and the Tanks game sample written exclusively in C#. At present, Ruan works as part of the development team for Crytek's award-winning entrance, into the free-to-play market, Warface, in Frankfurt.

> I'd like to thank my family, my friends in the industry with whom I've worked on some amazing side projects, and my wonderful girlfriend, Iulia, for supporting me constantly throughout the authoring of this book.

About the Reviewers

Terry Evans is a software developer with a degree from the University of Utah. He has a diverse background as a result of developing solutions in Unix, Linux, Windows, OS/2, Mac OS X, iOS, and Android, but has always enjoyed developing games the most during his career. He is the founder and currently lead developer for Entrada Interactive, which is developing a post-apocalyptic, multiplayer, survival game titled *Miscreated* using CryENGINE 3. Visit `MiscreatedGame.com` for more information on his latest venture.

Chris Parthemos is a recent entrant into the world of game development, but he has worked in developing content for AAA games for major studios. His educational background includes a Masters in Interactive Development from the Guildhall at Southern Methodist University, with a focus in Design and Scripting.

Hendrik Polczynski is a Software Developer from Germany. He has been working on software for over 10 years. He likes to take on a variety of different areas from industry automation to web, UI, and game development. You can find his open source projects at `github.com/hendrikp` or on his YouTube channel. Hendrik is maintaining a handful of open source projects around the CryDev community and the CryENGINE 3 FreeSDK. When Hendrik is not working, he is studying for his B.Sc. degree in Computer Science and Media Application, or helping out with the development of *Miscreated* by Entrada Interactive, which is a post-apocalyptic, survival-based MMORPG unlike anything you've played before.

Ross Rothenstine is an industry software engineer by day and hobbyist game programmer by night. He has a staunch reputation at his college for turning any major course project into a playable game by the end of it. He has a focus on Game Engine architecture and how complex subsystems come about in an elegant manner to make extensible, robust, and most importantly, fun to design games. This means quite a bit of time, reading, and coffee.

I would like to thank the authors of this book, as the content within it is pure, simple, and most of all, needed. In my days of wanting to learn CryENGINE programming, and reading the documents and code by hand, I had wished that a book like this would come about someday.

www.PacktPub.com

Support files, eBooks, discount offers and more

You might want to visit www.PacktPub.com for support files and downloads related to your book.

Did you know that Packt offers eBook versions of every book published, with PDF and ePub files available? You can upgrade to the eBook version at www.PacktPub.com and as a print book customer, you are entitled to a discount on the eBook copy. Get in touch with us at service@packtpub.com for more details.

At www.PacktPub.com, you can also read a collection of free technical articles, sign up for a range of free newsletters and receive exclusive discounts and offers on Packt books and eBooks.

http://PacktLib.PacktPub.com

Do you need instant solutions to your IT questions? PacktLib is Packt's online digital book library. Here, you can access, read and search across Packt's entire library of books.

Why Subscribe?

- Fully searchable across every book published by Packt
- Copy and paste, print and bookmark content
- On demand and accessible via web browser

Free Access for Packt account holders

If you have an account with Packt at www.PacktPub.com, you can use this to access PacktLib today and view nine entirely free books. Simply use your login credentials for immediate access.

Table of Contents

Preface

The process of developing and maintaining games has changed very rapidly in the last few years. It has become more and more common for game developers to license third-party game engines, such as CryENGINE, in order to focus fully on the game itself.

As the first game engine to ship with a pure **What You See Is What You Play (WYSIWYP)** philosophy in mind, CryENGINE focuses on productivity and iteration by allowing developers to jump directly into their games, previewing changes as they happen, and not waiting for levels and assets to build.

For a programmer, CryENGINE is the ideal toolset. Development can be done in C++ using the generous API, allowing developers to jump straight into the code and write high-performing code that is not limited to obscure scripting languages. Got an idea? Fire up Visual Studio and get right to work.

What this book covers

Chapter 1, *Introduction and Setup*, covers getting up to speed with a brief overview of the engine, detailing its strengths, the possibilities it provides, and a step-by-step guide to set up your environment.

Chapter 2, *Visual Scripting with Flowgraph*, introduces you to the visual scripting tool, giving an easy passage to create game logic in an accessible visual manner.

Chapter 3, *Creating and Utilizing Custom Entities*, covers the entity system and how to use it to your advantage. Populate your game world with entities that range from simple physicalized objects to complex weather simulation managers.

Chapter 4, *Game Rules*, provides you with an in-depth look into the game rules system, giving you a standardized template for overarching game and session logic. It also teaches how to implement your own custom game modes in a variety of languages.

Chapter 5, Creating Custom Actors, details the creation of custom actor classes for both player-controlled entities and the basis of artificial intelligence.

Chapter 6, Artificial Intelligence, covers the process of creating a living and breathing world by using the built-in artificial intelligence solution.

Chapter 7, The User Interface, details the process of using Flash and Autodesk Scaleform to spice up your interface with everything from simple on-screen bitmaps to rendering interactive flash elements in the game world.

Chapter 8, Multiplayer and Networking, covers the work behind taking the engine online, and learning how to synchronize the game world across the network.

Chapter 9, Physics Programming, covers the inner workings of the physics system, and the process of creating physical interactions for everything from the largest of vehicles to the smallest particle effect.

Chapter 10, Rendering Programming, helps you to learn how the rendering system works, and how to use it to create and expand everything from render nodes to multiple viewports.

Chapter 11, Effects and Sound, details the workings of the FMod sound engine in use by CryENGINE, allowing you to implement convincing sound for your project.

Chapter 12, Debugging and Profiling, covers common ways of debugging your game, and the basics of using the console.

What you need for this book

- CryENGINE 3 Free SDK v3.5.4
- CryMono v0.7 for CryENGINE 3.5.4
- Visual Studio Express 2012
- Notepad++
- FMod

Who this book is for

This book has been written for developers with a basic working knowledge of using CryENGINE and its Editor, and in some cases will assume the reader knows about very basic features such as loading a level in the Editor, and placing an entity. If you have never worked with CryENGINE before, we recommend either playing around with the CryENGINE Free SDK on your own, or purchasing *CryENGINE 3 Game Development: Beginner's Guide*, by *Sean Tracy* and *Paul Reindell*.

Conventions

In this book, you will find a number of styles of text that distinguish between different kinds of information. Here are some examples of these styles, and an explanation of their meaning.

Code words in text are shown as follows: "The GFx element determines which Flash file should be loaded for the element."

A block of code is set as follows:

```
<events>
  <event name="OnBigButton" fscommand="onBigButton"
    desc="Triggered when a big button is pressed">
    <param name="id" desc="Id of the button" type="string" />
  </event>
</events>

}
```

New terms and **important words** are shown in bold. Words that you see on the screen, in menus or dialog boxes for example, appear in the text like this: "Once started, the UI graph with the specified name will be activated, assuming it contains a **UI:Action:Start** node as shown:"

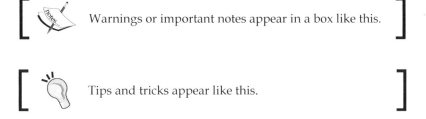

Warnings or important notes appear in a box like this.

Tips and tricks appear like this.

Reader feedback

Feedback from our readers is always welcome. Let us know what you think about this book—what you liked or may have disliked. Reader feedback is important for us to develop titles that you really get the most out of.

To send us general feedback, simply send an e-mail to `feedback@packtpub.com`, and mention the book title via the subject of your message.

If there is a topic that you have expertise in and you are interested in either writing or contributing to a book, see our author guide on `www.packtpub.com/authors`.

Customer support

Now that you are the proud owner of a Packt book, we have a number of things to help you to get the most from your purchase.

Errata

Although we have taken every care to ensure the accuracy of our content, mistakes do happen. If you find a mistake in one of our books—maybe a mistake in the text or the code—we would be grateful if you would report this to us. By doing so, you can save other readers from frustration and help us improve subsequent versions of this book. If you find any errata, please report them by visiting `http://www.packtpub.com/submit-errata`, selecting your book, clicking on the **errata submission form** link, and entering the details of your errata. Once your errata are verified, your submission will be accepted and the errata will be uploaded on our website, or added to any list of existing errata, under the Errata section of that title. Any existing errata can be viewed by selecting your title from `http://www.packtpub.com/support`.

Piracy

Piracy of copyright material on the Internet is an ongoing problem across all media. At Packt, we take the protection of our copyright and licenses very seriously. If you come across any illegal copies of our works, in any form, on the Internet, please provide us with the location address or website name immediately so that we can pursue a remedy.

Please contact us at copyright@packtpub.com with a link to the suspected pirated material.

We appreciate your help in protecting our authors, and our ability to bring you valuable content.

Questions

You can contact us at questions@packtpub.com if you are having a problem with any aspect of the book, and we will do our best to address it.

1
Introduction and Setup

CryENGINE is known as one of the most extensible engines available due to its ability to portray a vast variety of impressive visuals and gameplay. This makes it an invaluable tool at the hand of a programmer, where the only limit is one's creativity.

In this chapter, we will cover the following topics:

- Installing **Visual Studio Express 2012 for Windows Desktop**
- Downloading the CryENGINE sample installation or using a custom engine install
- Registering an account at `http://www.crydev.net`, the official CryENGINE development portal
- Compiling a stripped-down CryGame library
- Attaching and utilizing the debugger

Installing Visual Studio Express 2012

In order to compile the game code, you will need a copy of Visual Studio. For this demonstration, we'll be using Visual Studio Express 2012 for Windows Desktop.

 If you already have Visual Studio 2012 installed, you may skip this step.

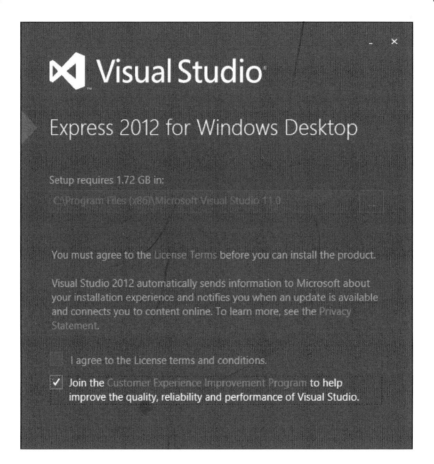

To install Visual Studio, follow the given steps:

1. Visit `http://www.microsoft.com/visualstudio/` and download Visual Studio Express 2012 for Windows Desktop.

2. After downloading the executable, install the application and proceed to the next step after restarting your computer.

Choosing your CryENGINE installation type

Now that we have Visual Studio installed, we'll need to download a version of CryENGINE to develop on.

We have created a stripped-down sample installation for the book, which is recommended for users who are just starting out with the engine. To download it, see the following *Downloading the book's CryENGINE sample installation* section.

If you would rather use another build of CryENGINE, such as the latest Free SDK release, please see the *Using a custom or newer CryENGINE installation* section later in this chapter. This section will cover integrating CryMono on your own.

Downloading the book's CryENGINE sample installation

For this book, we will be using a custom CryENGINE sample as a base for learning the workings of the engine. Most exercises in the book depend on this sample; however, the working knowledge you get from this can be applied to the default CryENGINE Free SDK (available at `http://www.crydev.net`).

To download the sample installation, follow these steps:

1. Visit `https://github.com/inkdev/CryENGINE-Game-Programming-Sample` and click on the **Download ZIP** button in order to download a compressed archive containing the sample.

2. Once downloaded, extract the contents of the archive to a folder of your choice. For the sake of the example, we will be extracting it to `C:\Crytek\CryENGINE-Programming-Sample`.

What just happened?

You should now have a copy of our sample CryENGINE installation. You can now run and view the sample content which we will be using for the most part of this book.

Using a custom or newer CryENGINE installation

This section helps out the readers who choose to use custom or newer builds of the engine. If you are unsure of this process, we recommend reading the *Downloading the book's CryENGINE sample installation* section in this chapter.

Verifying that the build is functional

Before starting, you should verify that your version of CryENGINE is functional so that you can use it for running and creating code based on this book's chapters.

 Note that if you are using an older or newer version of the engine, certain chapters may provide examples and information on changed systems. Keep this in mind, and refer to the sample mentioned previously for the optimal learning experience.

A good way to check this is by starting the Editor and Launcher applications and checking whether the engine behaves as expected.

Integrating CryMono (C# support)

If you're interested in using the sample code and chapter contents written with C# in mind, you'll need to integrate the third-party CryMono plugin into your CryENGINE installation.

 Note that CryMono is integrated by default in the sample we created specifically for this book.

To begin integrating CryMono, open the `Code` folder present in the engine root folder. We'll be placing the source files here, inside a subfolder called `CryMono/`.

To download the source code, visit `https://github.com/inkdev/CryMono` and click on **Download Zip** (or **Clone in Desktop** if you prefer using your Git revision control client).

Once downloaded, copy the contents into the `Code/CryMono` folder we mentioned earlier. If the folder does not exist, create it first.

When the files have been successfully moved, your folder structure should look similar to this:

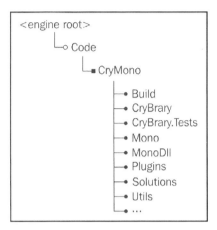

Compiling the CryMono project

Now that we have the CryMono source code, we'll need to compile it.

To start, open `Code/CryMono/Solutions/CryMono.sln` using Visual Studio.

> Make sure to use `CryMono.sln` and not `CryMono Full.sln`. The latter is only used when you need to rebuild the entire Mono runtime, which ships precompiled with the CryMono repository.

Before we compile, we'll need to modify the engine's `SSystemGlobalEnvironment` struct (this is exposed using the global `gEnv` pointer).

To do so, open `ISystem.h` in the `Code/CryEngine/CryCommon/` folder. Find the struct's definition by searching for the struct `SSystemGlobalEnvironment`.

Then add the following code to the very end of the struct's members and functions:

```
struct IMonoScriptSystem*
    pMonoScriptSystem;
```

Modifying interfaces is not recommended if you do not have full engine source, as other engine modules have been compiled with the default interfaces in mind. However, appending to the end of this struct is mostly harmless.

Once done, open up the instance of Visual Studio where you opened `CryMono.sln` and start compiling.

 The automated post-build step in the project should automatically move the compiled files to your build's `Bin32` folder following a successful compilation pass.

To verify that CryMono was compiled successfully, search for `CryMono.dll` in your `Bin32` folder.

Loading and initializing CryMono via the CryGame.dll library

Now that we have the CryMono binaries present in our `Bin32` folder, we'll just have to load it during game startup. This is done via the CryGame project, via the `CGameStartup` class.

To start, open your CryEngine or CryGame solution file (.sln) present in `Code/Solutions/`.

Including the CryMono interface folder

Before we modify the game startup code, we'll need to tell the compiler where to find the CryMono interfaces.

Start by right-clicking on the CryGame project in Visual Studio's **Solution Explorer** and select **Properties**. This should bring up the following **CryGame Property Pages** window:

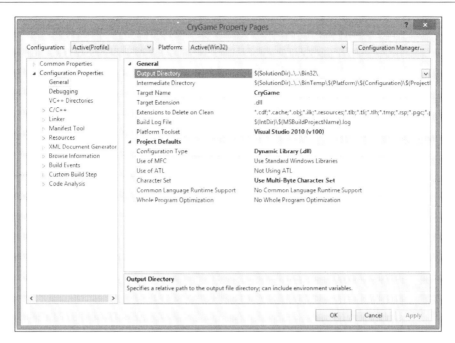

Now, click on **C/C++** and select **General**. This will bring up a screen of general compiler settings, which we'll use to add an additional include folder as shown in the following screenshot:

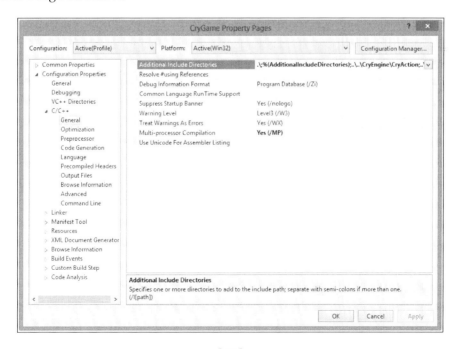

Now all we have to do is add `..\..\CryMono\MonoDll\Headers` to the **Additional Include Directories** menu. This will tell the compiler to search CryMono's `Headers` folder when the `#include` macro is used, allowing us to find the CryMono C++ interfaces.

Initializing CryMono at start up

Open `GameStartup.h` in the CryGame project and add the following to the bottom of the class declaration:

```
static HMODULE
m_cryMonoDll;
```

Then open `GameStartup.cpp` and add the following before the `CGameStartup` constructor:

```
HMODULE CGameStartup::m_cryMonoDll = 0;
```

Now navigate to the `CGameStartup` destructor and add the following code:

```
if(m_cryMonoDll)
{
  CryFreeLibrary(m_cryMonoDll);
  m_cryMonoDll = 0;
}
```

Now navigate to the `CGameStartup::Init` function declaration, and add the following prior to the `REGISTER_COMMAND("g_loadMod", RequestLoadMod, VF_NULL, "");` snippet:

```
m_cryMonoDll = CryLoadLibrary("CryMono.dll");
if(!m_cryMonoDll)
{
  CryFatalError("Could not locate CryMono DLL! %i",
    GetLastError());
  return false;
}

auto InitMonoFunc = (IMonoScriptSystem::
  TEntryFunction)CryGetProcAddress(m_cryMonoDll, "InitCryMono");
if(!InitMonoFunc)
{
  CryFatalError("Specified CryMono DLL is not valid!");
  return false;
}

InitMonoFunc(gEnv->pSystem, m_pFramework);
```

Now all we have to do is compile CryGame in order to have CryMono loaded and initialized at startup.

Registering flow nodes

Due to a recent change in the flow system, flow nodes have to be registered at a certain point during game startup. To make sure that our C# nodes are registered, we'll need to call `IMonoScriptSysetm::RegisterFlownodes` from `IGame::RegisterGameFlowNodes`.

To do this, open `Game.cpp` and add the following inside the `CGame::RegisterGameFlowNodes` function:

```
GetMonoScriptSystem()->RegisterFlownodes();
```

Now, after compiling, all managed flow nodes should appear in the Flowgraph Editor.

Registering your CryDev account

The CryENGINE Free SDK requires a CryDev account in order for the application's to launch. This can be easily retrieved via `http://www.crydev.net`, by following these steps:

1. Visit `http://www.crydev.net` in the browser of your choice.
2. Click on **Register** in the upper-right corner.
3. Read and accept the terms of usage.
4. Select your username data.

What just happened?

You now have your own CryDev user account. While running the CryENGINE Free SDK applications (see *Running the sample application*), you will be prompted to log in with the details you have just registered.

Running the sample application

Before we get started with building the game project, we'll go through the basics of the default CryENGINE applications.

All executables are contained inside either the `Bin32` or `Bin64` folders, depending on the build architecture. However, our sample only includes a `Bin32` folder to keep things simple and the build repository small in size.

Editor

This is the main application that developers will use. The Editor serves as the direct interface to the engine, used for all kinds of developer-specific tasks such as level design and character setup.

The Editor supports **WYSIWYP (What You See Is What You Play)** functionality, which allows developers to preview the game by hitting the shortcut *Ctrl + G*, or by navigating to the **Game** menu, and choosing **Switch to Game**.

Starting the Editor

Open the main sample folder, and navigate to the Bin32 folder. Once there, start Editor.exe.

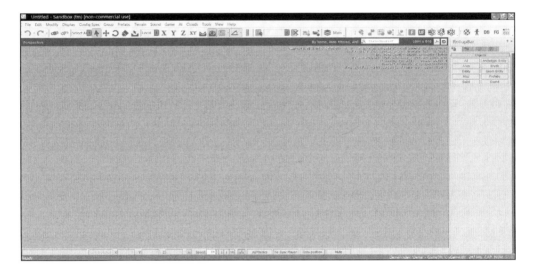

When the Editor has finished loading, you will be greeted by the Sandbox interface, which can be used to create most visual aspects of the game (excluding models and textures).

To create a new level, open the **File** menu, and select the **New** option. This should present you with the **New Level** message box. Simply specify your level name and click on **OK**, and the Editor will create and load your empty level.

To load an existing level, open the **File** menu, and select the **Open** option. This presents you with the **Open Level** message box. Select your level and click on **Open** to have your level loaded.

Launcher

This is the application seen by the end user. Upon startup, the Launcher displays the game's main menu, along with different options allowing users to load levels and configure the game.

The Launcher's game context is commonly referred to as **Pure game mode**.

Starting the Launcher

Open the main sample folder, and navigate into the Bin32 folder. Once there, start Launcher.exe.

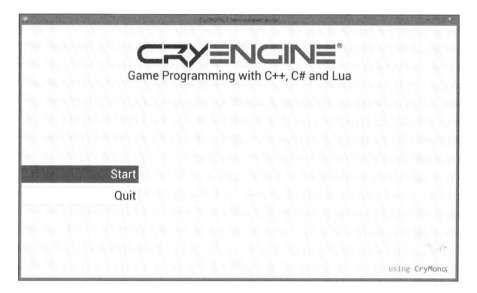

When you've started the application, you'll be greeted with the default main menu. This interface allows the user to load levels and alter game settings such as visuals and controls.

The Launcher is preferable over the Editor when you want to play the game as the end user would. Another benefit is the quick startup time.

Dedicated server

The dedicated server is used to start up a multiplayer server for other clients to connect to. The dedicated server does not initialize a renderer, and instead functions as a console application.

```
D:\Dev\INK\Tanks\Bin32\DedicatedServer.exe                               □   x
                      CryEngine - Dedicated Server - Version 3.4.3.5047
[Lobby] Initialise service 1 error 2
[Error] Failed to initialise CryLobby in Game. Return value is 0x2
GameWarning trying to display: LobbyStartFailed
CGameLobby::CGameLobby()
Loading Localization File Localization\text_ui_ingame.xml
Loading Localization File Localization\text_ui_menus.xml
Loading Localization File Localization\text_ui_levels.xml
Loading Localization File Localization\text_ui_warnings.xml
Create AG musiclogic.xml
Release AG musiclogic.xml
[Warning] XML reader: Can't open file (Animations/graphs/musiclogic.xml)
Error parsing <Animations/graphs/musiclogic.xml>: XML reader: Can't open file (Animations/graphs/musiclogic.xml)
[Warning] Unable to load music logic graph
Ending game context...
[Warning] [Lua Error] Failed to load script file Scripts/GameRules/DeathMatch.lua
[Warning] [Lua Error] Failed to load script file Scripts/Entities/Default/GeomEntity.lua
[Warning] [Lua Error] Failed to load script file Scripts/Entities/Default/RopeEntity.lua
[Warning] [Lua Error] Failed to load script file Scripts/GameRules/SinglePlayer.lua
[Warning] [Lua Error] Failed to load script file Scripts/Entities/Actor/Tank.lua
[Warning] [Lua Error] Failed to load script file Scripts/Entities/Vehicles/VehiclePartDetached.lua
[Warning] [flow] Attempt to link an output node to an output node
[Warning] [flow] Attempt to link an output node to an output node
[Warning] [flow] Trying to link an invalid node
[Warning] [flow] Attempt to link an output node to an output node
[Warning] [flow] Attempt to link an output node to an output node
[Warning] [flow] Attempt to link an output node to an output node
[Warning] [flow] <noname> : Can't link edge <13,Explode> to <4,Disable> - FLOWGRAPH DISCARDED
[Warning] [flow] <noname> : Did not load all edges (8/13 edges) - FLOWGRAPH DISCARDED
[Warning] [Lua Error] Failed to load script file scripts/main.lua
[Warning] [CScriptSystem::BeginCall] Function OnInit not found(check for syntax errors or if the file wasn't loaded)
pm_listsi
[CONSOLE] Executing console command 'pm_listsi'
[Manager_Plugin] Currently 0 static interfaces are registered!
pm_list
[CONSOLE] Executing console command 'pm_list'
[Manager_Plugin] CryMono: V(0.7-dev) C(Framework) S(Undefined) U(false) I(true) FI(true) F(CryMono.dll) D(D:\Dev\INK\Ta\
nks\Bin32\Plugins\CryMono) M(133E0000) B(1345D448)
[Manager_Plugin] Manager: V(1.1.0.0) C(General) S(OK) U(false) I(true) FI(true) F(Plugin_Manager.dll) D(D:\Dev\INK\Tank\
s\Bin32\Plugins) M(53DE0000) B(53DFAA38)
[Manager_Plugin] Currently 2 plugins are loaded!
exec autoexec.cfg
[CONSOLE] Executing console command 'exec autoexec.cfg'
Executing console batch file (try game.config.root): "autoexec.cfg" not found!
:::::::::  is loaded in 453522.9 sec :::::::::
Textures startup streaming finished in 0.3 sec
Average block size: 0 KB, Average throughput: 0.0 MB/sec, Jobs processed: 0 (0.0 MB), File IO Bandwidth: 0.00MB/s
  map:nolevel rules:DeathMatch                    | upd:0.1ms(0.03..0.14) rate:34.2/s up:0.0k/s dn: 0.0k/s
]
```

Compiling the CryGame project (C++)

The CryENGINE Free SDK ships with complete source access to the game logic library, CryGame.dll. This dynamic library is responsible for the main part of game features, as well as the initial game startup process.

A library is *a collection of existing classes and functions that can be integrated into other projects. In Windows, the most common form of library is* a **Dynamic Link Library**, or **DLL**, *which uses the* .dll *file extension.*

To start off, open the main sample folder, and navigate to Code/Solutions/, in which a Visual Studio solution file named CE Game Programming Sample. sln should be present. Double-click on the file and Visual Studio should start up, displaying the included projects (see the following breakdown).

 A **solution** is a structure for organizing projects in Visual Studio. The **solution** contains information on projects in a text-based .sln file, as well as a .suo file (user-specific options).

To build the project, simply press *F7* or right-click on the CryGame project in the **Solution Explorer** and select **Build**.

What just happened?

You just compiled CryGame.dll, which should now be present in the binary folder. (Bin32 for 32-bit compilation, Bin64 for 64-bit). Launching the sample application will now load the .dll file containing the source code you compiled.

The CE Game Programming Sample solution breakdown

The solution includes the following three projects, one of which compiles to a .dll file.

CryGame

The CryGame project includes the underlying game logic used by the engine. This compiles to CryGame.dll.

CryAction

The CryAction project includes partial source to CryAction.dll, which is responsible for a large number of systems, such as actors, UI Graphs, and game objects. This project does not compile to a .dll file, but is instead only used for interface access.

CryCommon

The CryCommon project is a helper containing all shared CryENGINE interfaces. If there is a subsystem you want access to, look for its exposed interface in here.

The CryENGINE folder structure

See the following table for an explanation of the CryENGINE folder structure:

Folder name	Description
Bin32	Contains all 32-bit executables and libraries used by the engine.
Bin64	Contains all 64-bit executables and libraries used by the engine.
Editor	Editor configuration folder, contains common editor helpers, styles, and more.
Engine	Used as a central folder for assets used by the engine itself, not any particular game.
	Shaders and configuration files are stored here.
Game	Each game contains a game folder, which includes all its assets, scripts, levels, and so on.
	Does not have to be named "Game", but is dependent on the value of the sys_game_ folder console variable.
Localization	Contains localization assets such as localized sounds and text for each language.

PAK files

The engine ships with the **CryPak** module, allowing for the storage of game content files in compressed or uncompressed archives. The archives use the .pak file extension.

When game content is requested, the CryPak system will query through all found .pak files in order to find the file.

File query priority

The PAK system prioritizes the files found in the loose folder structure over those in PAK, except when the engine was compiled in RELEASE mode. When that is the case, the file stored in a PAK system is preferred over the loose one.

If the file exists in multiple .pak archives, the one with the most recent filesystem creation date is used.

Attaching the debugger

Visual Studio allows you to attach the **Debugger** to your application. This allows you to use functionalities such as **breakpoints**; letting you stop at a specific line in your C++ source code, and step through the program execution.

To start debugging, open `CE Game Programming Sample.sln` and press *F5*, or click on the green play icon on the Visual Studio toolbar. If a **No debug symbols could be found for Editor.exe** message box appears, simply click on **OK**.

What just happened?

The CryENGINE Sandbox editor should now have started, with the Visual Studio Debugger attached. We can now place breakpoints in code, and watch program execution pause when that specific line of code is executed.

Summary

In this chapter, we have downloaded and learned how to use a CryENGINE installation. You should now be aware of the process of compiling and debugging the CryGame project.

We now have the basic knowledge needed to move on to learning the ins and outs of the CryENGINE programming API.

If you feel like learning more about CryENGINE itself, besides programming knowledge, feel free to start the Sandbox editor and play around with the level design tools. This will help you prepare for future chapters, where you'll be required to utilize the Editor Viewport and more.

2
Visual Scripting with Flowgraph

The CryENGINE flowgraph is a powerful node-based visual scripting system, aiding developers in rapidly prototyping features and creating level specific logic without having to work with complicated codebases.

In this chapter, we will:

- Discuss the concept of flowgraphs
- Create new flowgraphs
- Debug our flowgraph
- Create a custom flowgraph node (flownode) in Lua, C#, and C++

Concept of flowgraphs

For years, writing code has been the primary, if not the exclusive method of creating behaviors and logic for games. Let's take the example of a level designer, building a combat section for the latest title.

Traditionally, the said designer would have to ask a programmer to create the logic for this scenario. This has several problems:

- It creates a disconnect between the design and the implementation
- Programmers are forced into spending time which is really a designer's job
- The designer has no immediate feedback on how his/her section plays out

This is the problem that CryENGINE's **flowgraph**, often referred to as **FG**, solves. It provides a set of flownodes, best thought of as convenient Lego blocks of logic, which the designer can utilize to piece together entire scenarios. No more requests to the game code team; designers can go ahead and realize their ideas instantly! We'll discuss creating the nodes themselves in more detail later, but for now, let's take a look at some simple flowgraphs, so you can take your first steps into CryENGINE game logic!

Opening the Flowgraph Editor

To get started, we need to open up Sandbox. Sandbox contains the Flowgraph Editor as one of its many useful tools, and it can be opened via **View | Open View Pane**.

 You should always have a level loaded when opening the Flowgraph Editor, as flowgraphs are unique to levels. Flick back to *Chapter 1, Introduction and Setup*, if you've forgotten how to create a new level!

You've just accessed your first Sandbox tool! You should be presented with a new window with lots of subsections and features, but don't fret, let's tackle them one by one.

A tour of the Flowgraph Editor

Flowgraphs are saved on the disk as XML files, but can be parsed and edited by the Flowgraph Editor in order to provide a visual interface to the process of creating game logic.

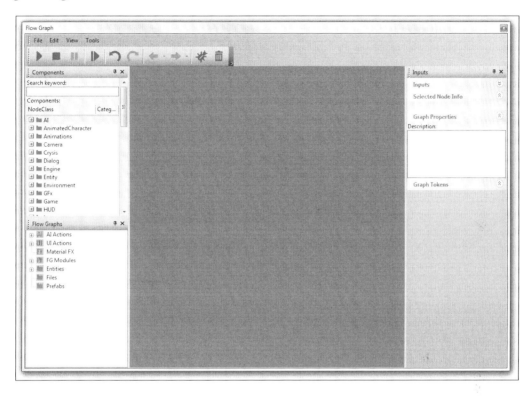

Components

This section of the Editor contains all the flownodes in your project, organized into neat categories. Let's take a quick look inside this, open up the **Misc** folder. You should be presented with a set of nodes, assigned to categories:

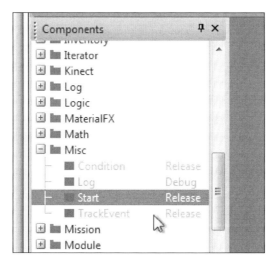

Terminology

- **Graph**: This refers to a context containing a set of nodes linked to each other.

- **Node**: This is a visual representation of a class that can receive data and events from its input ports, as well as send data via its output ports. It is connected to other nodes in graphs to create logic.

- **Port**: This is a visual representation of a function. Nodes can specify multiple input and output ports, and can then send or receive events from them.

Component categories

You may be missing the node marked as **Debug** here; CryENGINE assigns categories to nodes as a way of indicating where it's appropriate for them to be used.

- **Release**: This node is suitable for use in production

- **Advanced**: While this node is suitable for use in production, it may have complex behavior in certain situations

- **Debug**: This node should only be used for internal tests

- **Obsolete**: This node should not be used, and this node will not be visible in the components list

For example, while working on a level that's intended to be shipped to the public, you might not want to accidentally include any Debug nodes! We can enable or disable the viewing of the first three categories inside the Flowgraph Editor via **View | Components**:

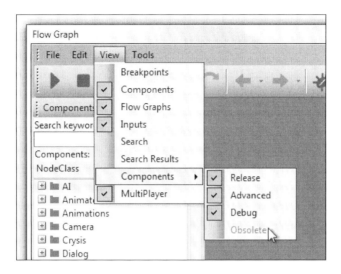

Flowgraph types

Before creating a new flowgraph, we'll want to know of what type our purpose is most relevant to. Different flowgraph types allow for specialization, for example, to create **UI graphs** that handle the layout and drawing of the player's user interface.

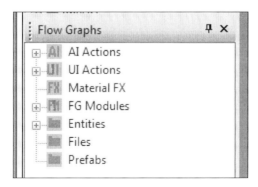

AI Actions

These are flowgraphs you can create to wrap up AI behaviors into convenient nodes that can be reused elsewhere. We'll address these later when you learn about **Artificial Intelligence (AI)**.

UI Actions

CryENGINE allows you to script your user interfaces and in-game heads-up-displays using flowgraphs, via a system of UI events. We'll discuss these in *Chapter 7, The User Interface*.

Material FX

CryENGINE supports convenient designer-editable flowgraphs to control how material events are handled, for example, spawning a dirt particle and obscuring the player's screen with a layer of dust when the ground is shot nearby.

FG Modules

You can package up flowgraphs into handy modules for reuse across different situations. We'll describe these in depth later.

Entities

This is where we'll spend most of our time in this chapter! 90 percent of the time, a flowgraph is assigned to an entity, otherwise known as the **graph entity**, and this logic takes place in the game world.

Prefabs

CryENGINE supports prefabs, a collection of entities packaged into a single convenient file for reuse. Any entity flowgraphs inside a prefab will be displayed in this folder.

Creating a flowgraph

Now that we have a basic understanding of how the Flowgraph Editor works, let's dive right in and create our first flowgraph! You can close the Flowgraph Editor for the moment.

The flowgraph entity

The flowgraph entity is an extremely lightweight CryENGINE object, designed to be used when you need a flowgraph that isn't applied to any specific entity. Like all entities, it can be found in **RollupBar** inside Sandbox.

 If you're not sure what an entity is, skip this section until you have read *Chapter 3, Creating and Utilizing Custom Entities.*

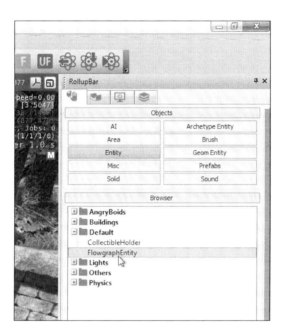

Spawning FlowgraphEntity

Select **FlowgraphEntity** and then either double-click and click again on the viewport, or click and drag it into the level. You should now see a whole new set of options in **RollupBar**, including entity params, material layers, but mostly important for us, the **Entity: FlowgraphEntity** section.

Attaching a new flowgraph

Inside the **Entity: FlowgraphEntity** section, we need to find the **Flow Graph** subsection, and then click on the **Create** button:

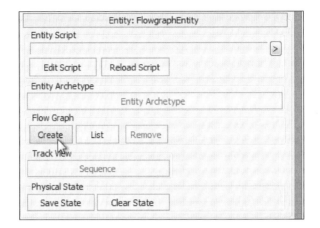

From here, you'll be presented with the option to assign your flowgraph to a group. Whether you do or not isn't really important for now, but it's useful for grouping related graphs together, particularly when working on larger projects.

 Groups are used to create a structure for flowgraphs, allowing developers to sort different graphs into folders.

Once this is done, you should see the Flowgraph Editor appear with a faint grid overlaid on the background. We're now ready to start creating logic!

Adding nodes into flowgraphs

The simplest method of adding a node into a new graph is to browse through the **Components** list and drag new nodes in. However, this isn't very efficient if you know the name of the node you want to add. Therefore, you can also use the *Q* shortcut key inside the Flowgraph Editor to bring up the search function, and just type in the name of the node you'd like to add.

In our case, we're going to begin with the **Misc:Start** node, which is a simple node used to set off other events when the level is loaded, or when an Editor test session is started:

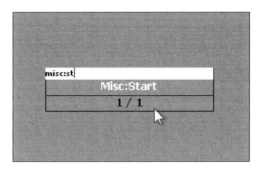

Input and output ports

Once the node is placed, you should see your first example of a node's input and output ports. In this case, we have two input values, **InGame** and **InEditor**, as well as a single output port, conveniently named **output** in this case:

Input ports are used to feed data into the node, or trigger events, and output ports are used to relay data and events to other nodes in the graph. In this example, the **Misc:Start** node can be edited to define in which game contexts it will actually be executed. Perhaps you have some debugging logic you'd like to only run in the Editor, in which case we could set **InGame** to false, or zero.

Port types

In order to specify what type of data a port will handle, we need to know its port type. We can tell which type a port is in the Flowgraph Editor by looking at its color.

Following is a list of the available port types:

- **Void**: This is used for ports that don't pass a specific value, but are activated to signal an event
- **Int**: This is used when the port should only receive integer values
- **Float**: This is used to indicate that the port handles floating point values

- **EntityId**: This indicates that the port expects an entity identifier. (Refer to *Chapter 3, Creating and Utilizing Custom Entities* for more information on entity IDs)

- **Vec3**: This is used for ports that handle three-dimensional vectors

- **String**: In this, the port expects a string

- **Bool**: This is used when the port expects a Boolean value of true or false

 Linking ports with different types will result in the value being automatically converted.

Target entities

Flownodes can feature a target entity, allowing the user to link an entity from the current level to the flownode. This is useful for nodes that are meant to impact entities in the game world, for example the **Entity:GetPos** node, as shown in the following screenshot, gets the world transformation of the specified entity.

 We can also specify entities dynamically by linking an **EntityId** output port to the **Choose Entity** port.

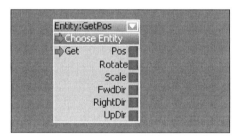

There are two ways of assigning an entity to a node that supports it:

- By linking another flownodes' **EntityId** output to the **Choose Entity** input

- By right-clicking on the **Choose Entity** input and selecting:

   ○ **Assign selected entity**: This links the node to the entity currently selected in the Editor viewport

   ○ **Assign graph entity**: This links the node to the entity this graph is assigned to

Linking flownodes

A single flownode isn't capable of much; let's connect two, and build a proper graph! For demonstration purposes, we'll use the **Time:TimeOfDay** node:

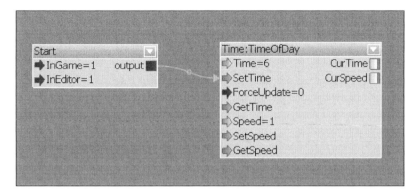

To create a link between ports as shown in the previous screenshot, simply click on an output port and drag your cursor to an input port with the mouse button held down. Release the mouse, and the connection should be created!

We've also edited the value of the **Time** input port; input ports can either be fed data via output ports, or have their values edited directly in the Editor. To do this, just click on the node and see the **Inputs** section of the Flowgraph Editor. From there, you can simply edit the values:

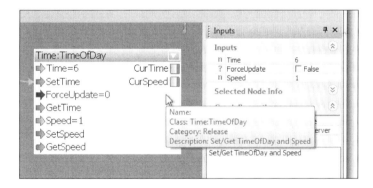

You can also see valuable information about the node: for example, here we can see that this node is used to set the time of day, and the speed at which time passes in game.

With this done, you can close the Flowgraph Editor for now. Flowgraphs don't have to be saved manually; they're automatically saved with the level.

 Although flowgraphs save with the level, it is good practice to save manually often using **File** | **Save** to avoid losing your work.

Testing our flowgraph

As we learned in the previous chapter, testing logic in the CryENGINE is incredibly simple using Sandbox. Simply press the *Ctrl + G* shortcut key combination, and watch as you enter game mode. Now, when you do this, you should see the lighting and general atmosphere of the level changing, as you've just changed the time of day!

Congratulations, you've just taken your first step to creating games using CryENGINE! It doesn't seem like much right now, but let's make this graph do a bit more.

The stock flownode overview

To make something a little more complex, we're going to need an understanding of what nodes the CryENGINE provides for us by default.

Building a clock

One of the most useful nodes we have access to, at least for debugging purposes, is the **HUD:DisplayDebugMessage** node. It allows you to display information in the game window, optionally with a timeout. With that in mind, let's build a little debug clock based on the time information we learnt about earlier.

The **Time:TimeOfDay** node outputs the current time in the CryENGINE time format, which is defined as hours plus minutes divided by 60. For example, 1:30 p.m. would be expressed as 13.5 in CryENGINE time. We now know we're going to need some mathematical operations, so it's time to check the Math flownode category.

The first thing we'll do is get the time in hours by rounding the current time down. To do this, place **Math:Floor**, then connect the **CurTime** output from our **Time:TimeOfDay** node to Floor's **A** input port. Then, feed this into a Debug Message node:

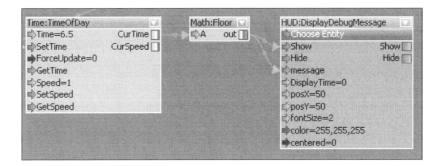

Jump into game right now, and you should see the current time in hours displayed on your screen.

We then need to subtract our new value from our original to get the minutes portion. To do this, we need **Math:Sub** to subtract the rounded hours from the original **CurTime** value. After that, a **Math:Mul** node will scale up the new time by 60, so your graph should look like this:

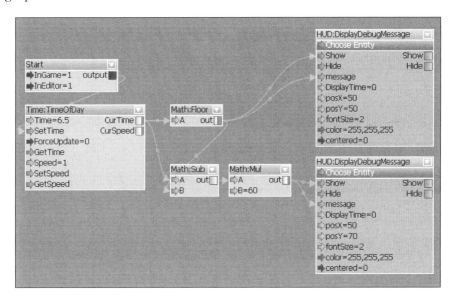

Remember to set **posY** of the second Debug node to move it down which will enable you to see both at the same time.

If you jump in game again, you should now see the current hours and minutes printed!

Listening for player input

What if now, we wanted to allow the player to test moving through different times of the day? Generally speaking, it's the easiest way to set up a key listener, where we fire an event when a certain key is pressed. Fortunately CryENGINE encapsulates this functionality nicely into a single node, **Input:Key**.

Let's now set it up so that pressing the *P* key will make time move extremely fast, and that pressing *O* will stop it again.

 The **Input:Key** node is a Debug node. It is generally considered a bad practice to use Debug nodes in production, as unexpected results may occur, so please don't use this node for actual game logic.

We need to set the **Speed** value of our **Time:TimeOfDay** node, but in this case, we'll also need to feed two values in! CryENGINE provides a node called **Logic:Any** that features multiple input ports and just passes on any data given to it, which we can use here to receive both input values. We use two key nodes which call **Math:SetNumber** nodes, and the **Logic:Any** node then relays this information to our **Time:TimeOfDay** node, as well as calling **SetSpeed**:

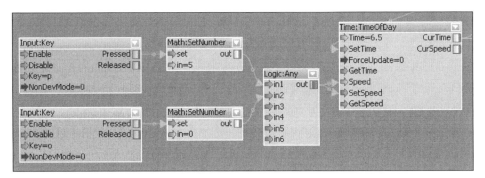

Jump in game now, and press *P* to start the day moving! Press *O* again, and the time of day should freeze.

Executing on a loop

You might have noticed that our clock isn't updating correctly any more. This is because most nodes won't output data unless triggered; in this case, we'll get no output if we don't trigger either **GetTime** or **SetTime**. We have two options for calling this: we can either use **Time:Time** to execute it every frame, or **Time:Timer**.

The latter can control the granularity of the tick, but in this case, we probably want it to be updated every frame while moving fast, so let's keep it simple. Connect the **tick** output to our **GetTime** input, and our clock should be updating correctly once again!

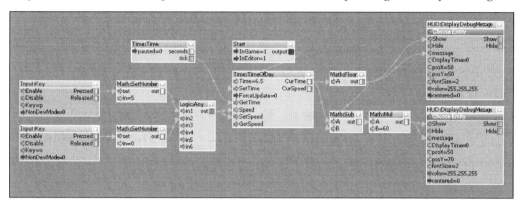

Flowgraph modules

The flowgraph module system allows flowgraphs to be exported as a module that can be triggered from another graph.

By creating modules, we can reuse logic in multiple levels without having to maintain several versions of the same graph. It's also possible to send and receive unique data to and from the modules, allowing dynamic logic in a very modular manner.

Creating a module

To start with creating your own module, open the Flowgraph Editor and select **File | New FG Module... | Global**:

In the resulting **Save** dialog box, save the module with a name of your choice. You'll then be shown the default view of a module:

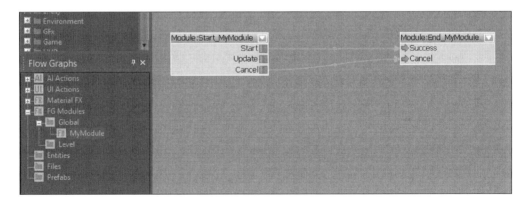

The module contains two nodes by default; **Module:Start_MyModule** and **Module:End_MyModule**.

- **Module:Start_MyModule** contains three output ports:
  - **Start**: This is called when the module is loaded

- ○ **Update**: This is called when the module should be updated

- ○ **Cancel**: This is called when the module should cancel, and it is connected to the **Cancel** input of **Module:End_MyModule** by default

- **Module:End_MyModule** contains two input ports:

  - ○ **Success**: This should be called when finalizing the module, and passes a "success" status to the caller

  - ○ **Cancel**: This is used to end the module prematurely, and passes a "cancelled" status to the caller

Finally, to fill your module with logic, simply connect the **Start** output port to your logic nodes.

Calling a module

To call an existing module, find the relevant node in the Module node category. The call nodes are named as `Module:Call_<ModuleName>`:

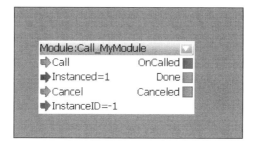

Then simply trigger the **Call** port to activate your module, and **Cancel** to abort it.

Module parameters/ports

From what we've learned previously, we're able to call modules with a void port. This is not optimal in all cases, as you might want to pass additional data to the module.

To allow this, the module system exposes module parameters. By selecting **Tools |
Edit Module...** in the Flowgraph Editor, we can add a set of parameters to our module:

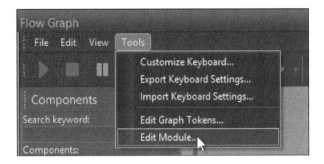

This action opens the **Module Ports** window, which allows us to add and
remove ports:

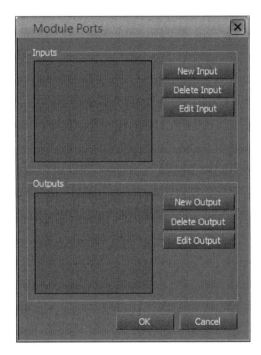

By selecting **New Input** or **New Output**, we'll be able to add new ports that can be
used when activating the module.

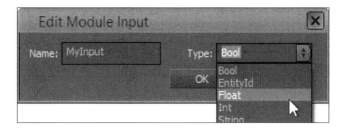

Adding a new input or output will automatically output its **Module:Start_ MyModule** or **Module:End_MyModule** node, allowing you to receive the data:

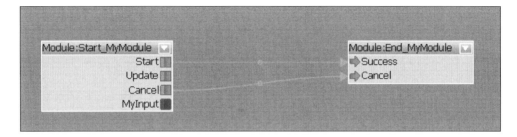

All **Module:Call_MyModule** nodes are also updated automatically, giving you access to the new parameter right away:

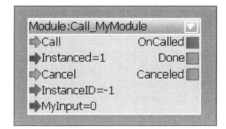

Custom flownodes

To summarize, CryENGINE provides many useful nodes by default, encompassing a whole range of functionality. However, as a programmer, you'll often find that designers will request access to some hidden functionality that the flowgraph isn't capable of providing by default.

For example, let's say you're creating a role-playing game, and you have an experience system. There are plenty of ways to reward the player with experience in the code you've written, but a level designer also wants to be able to make use of this functionality at arbitrary points in a level.

In this situation, you're well-placed to create a custom flownode; you can create a simplified representation of the system that exists in code, perhaps allowing the designer to simply specify the number of experience points to award to the player when the node is triggered.

For now though, we're going to take a look at something a little simpler. Let's pretend we have no existing CryENGINE nodes to work with, and we'd like to implement the **Math:Mul** node we saw earlier. To recap, it's just a simple node that implements multiplication inside a flowgraph.

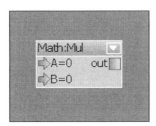

Creating a custom node in C++

Back in *Chapter 1, Introduction and Setup*, we took a first look at compiling and running the GameDLL, packaged here as `MiniMonoGameSample.sln` for Visual Studio. Let's load that up again, making sure that any CryENGINE instances such as the Launcher or Sandbox are closed, as we're going to overwrite the `CryGame.dll` file that's used at runtime.

Organizing nodes

The standard practice for CryENGINE games is to have a filter in the GameDLL project, **CryGame**, called **Nodes**. If this doesn't exist, go ahead and create it now.

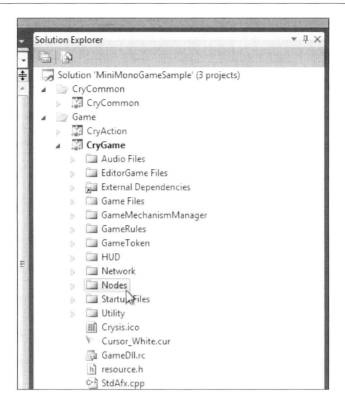

Creating a new node file

Nodes are never referenced in other areas of the project, so it's fine to simply implement a node as a single .cpp file without a header.

In our case, let's just add a new file, TutorialNode.cpp, and create the basic structure:

```
#include "stdafx.h"
#include "Nodes/G2FlowBaseNode.h"

    class CTutorialNode : public CFlowBaseNode<eNCT_Instanced>
    {

    };

    REGISTER_FLOW_NODE("Tutorial:Multiplier", CTutorialNode);
```

Breaking down of code

Firstly, we included `stdafx.h`; this provides common functionality and some standardized "includes" for your file. This is also required to compile files.

After that, we included a second file, `Nodes/G2FlowBaseNode.h`. While it's not strictly a CryENGINE component, this file is widely used in CryENGINE games to encapsulate node functionality into an easily accessible base class.

We then create our actual class definition. We inherit from the aforementioned base node, and then specify that our node is an instanced node; generally speaking, you'll work with instanced nodes in CryENGINE.

> CryENGINE uses some limited Hungarian notation prefixes as you see here. Classes are `CMyClass`, structs become `SMyData`, and interfaces are `IMyInterface`.
>
> It's also common to use the `m_` prefix for fields, such as `m_memberVariable`, and p for pointer variables, such as `*pAnInstance`.

In order to make node registration easier, CryENGINE exposes `REGISTER_FLOW_NODE` pre-processor macro. This system will automatically handle registration of your node during startup.

The node functions overview

For the purposes of the node we are creating, we don't need to store any private information, so simply make all node information public using the C++ modifier as the first line inside your class:

```
public:
```

We then start off by implementing two functions, the constructor and the `Clone` method. We don't need any logic in either of these, so the implementations are very simple; the constructor doesn't initialize anything, and `Clone` simply returns a new instance of the current node:

```
CTutorialNode(SActivationInfo *pActInfo)
{
}

virtual IFlowNodePtr Clone(SActivationInfo *pActInfo)
{
  return new CTutorialNode(pActInfo);
}
```

Here, we're also introduced to SActivationInfo for the first time. This struct contains information about the node's present state, as well as the graph it's contained within, and we'll be using this elsewhere later.

Now, three more functions are required for our node to at least compile:

```
virtual void ProcessEvent(EFlowEvent evt, SActivationInfo
  *pActInfo)
{
}

virtual void GetConfiguration(SFlowNodeConfig &config)
{
}

virtual void GetMemoryUsage(ICrySizer *s) const
{
  s->Add(*this);
}
```

ProcessEvent is where we'll be doing most of our node logic; this function is called when interesting things happen to our node, such as ports being triggered. GetConfiguration controls how the node will be displayed, as well as what input and output ports it contains. GetMemoryUsage doesn't need any extra implementation from us, so we can just add a reference to this node for memory usage tracking.

Now, it would be a good point to verify that your code compiles; if not, check whether you've declared all the function signatures correctly, and included the headers.

Implementing GetConfiguration

As mentioned earlier, GetConfiguration is where we set up how our node can be used in the Flowgraph Editor. Firstly, let's set up enum to describe our input ports; we're going to use two values, left and right, as well as an activation port to trigger the calculation. Declare this inside the class:

```
enum EInput
{
  EIP_Activate,
  EIP_Left,
  EIP_Right
};
```

Of course, we also need an output port for the calculation, so let's create enum with a single value for that also. It's not required, but it's a good practice to be consistent, and most nodes will have more than one output:

```
enum EOutput
{
   EOP_Result
};
```

Creating ports

With those declared, we can start building up our node. Ports are defined as entries in a constant static array declared in GetConfiguration, and are constructed using some helper functions, namely InputPortConfig<T> for a specific type of value, as well as InputPortConfig_AnyType for allowing all values, and InputPortConfig_Void for ports that use no data.

With that in mind, we know that a void input will be required for our trigger input on top of two float templated ports. We'll also need a float output.

```
virtual void GetConfiguration(SFlowNodeConfig &config)
{
   static const SInputPortConfig inputs[] =
   {
     InputPortConfig_Void("Activate", "Triggers the
       calculation"),
     InputPortConfig<float>("Left", 0, "The left side of the
       calculation"),
     InputPortConfig<float>("Right", 0, "The right side of the
       calculation"),
     {0}
   };
}
```

As you can see, we get to specify the name of the port, the description, as well as a default value for ports that use data. They should match the order of the enums that we declared earlier.

 Changing port names for nodes that are already used will break existing graphs. Fill in the optional humanName parameter to change the display name.

Now we repeat that process, except we use the output set of functions:

```
static const SOutputPortConfig outputs[] =
{
  OutputPortConfig<float>("Result", "The result of the
    calculation"),
  {0}
};
```

Assigning arrays to the node configuration

Following the process of creating our ports, we need to assign these arrays to our `config` parameter, as well as provide a description and category:

```
config.pInputPorts = inputs;
config.pOutputPorts = outputs;
config.sDescription = _HELP("Multiplies two numbers");
config.SetCategory(EFLN_APPROVED);
```

If you compile the code now, the node should be fully visible in the Editor. But as you'll see, it does nothing yet; to fix that, we have to implement `ProcessEvent`!

Flownode configuration flags

The `SFlowNodeConfig` struct allows you to assign optional flags to the flownode, listed as shown:

- `EFLN_TARGET_ENTITY`: This is used to indicate that this node should support a target entity. To obtain the currently assigned target entity, have a look at `SActivationInfo::pEntity`.

- `EFLN_HIDE_UI`: This hides the node from the user in the flowgraph UI.

- `EFLN_UNREMOVEABLE`: This disables the ability for the user to remove the node.

To append a flag within `GetConfiguration`, in this case to support a target entity, simply add the flag to the `nFlags` variable:

```
config.nFlags |= EFLN_TARGET_ENTITY;
```

Implementing ProcessEvent

`ProcessEvent` is where we catch all the interesting events for our node, such as ports being triggered. In our case, we want to perform a calculation whenever our `Activate` port is triggered, so we need to check for port activations. First though, we can save ourselves some processing by checking which event we'd like to handle.

```
virtual void ProcessEvent(EFlowEvent evt, SActivationInfo
  *pActInfo)
{
  switch (evt)
  {
    case eFE_Activate:
    {

    }
    break;
  }
}
```

Usually you'll be handling more than one event, so it's good to get into the habit of using a `switch` statement here.

Inside that, let's take a look at the various flownode functions we use to check for activations, to retrieve data, and then trigger an output:

```
if (IsPortActive(pActInfo, EIP_Activate))
{
  float left = GetPortFloat(pActInfo, EIP_Left);
  float right = GetPortFloat(pActInfo, EIP_Right);
  float answer = left * right;

  ActivateOutput(pActInfo, EOP_Result, answer);
}
```

To summarize, we use our activation information in all these functions to represent the current state. We can then retrieve values using the `GetPort*` functions for the various port types, and then trigger an output with data.

It's time to load up the Editor and test; if all's gone well, you should be able to see your node in the Tutorial category. Congratulations, you've just written your first C++ code for CryENGINE!

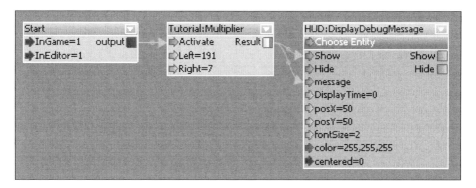

Creating a custom node in C#

CryMono also supports the creation of custom nodes using idioms that C# developers will feel accustomed to, such as attribute metaprogramming. To get started with C# CryENGINE scripts, open up the sample scripts solution in `Game/Scripts/CryGameCode.sln`. Add a new `.cs` file to the flownodes folder, and we'll start creating the same node in C#, so you can see how the creation varies.

To start with, let's create a basic skeleton node. We need to bring the correct namespace into scope for the `Flowgraph` classes, as well as set up some basic attributes for our node:

```
using CryEngine.Flowgraph;

namespace CryGameCode.FlowNodes
{
   [FlowNode(Name = "Multiplier", Category = "CSharpTutorial",
     Filter = FlowNodeFilter.Approved)]
   public class TutorialNode : FlowNode
   {

   }
}
```

As in C++, nodes aren't referenced anywhere else in the project, so we assign a separate namespace for our nodes to keep them from polluting the main namespaces.

We use the `FlowNodeAttribute` class in place of `GetConfiguration` to set up metadata for our node, such as the correct category and visibility level. Your node must include this attribute and inherit it from `FlowNode` in order to be registered by the CryENGINE; there's no need for any manual registration calls.

 Remember that attributes can be placed without the last `Attribute` of its name. For example, `FlowNodeAttribute` can be placed as both `[FlowNodeAttribute]` and `[FlowNode]`.

Adding inputs

Inputs are defined as functions in CryMono, and they take either a single parameter which defines the data type, or no parameter for void ports. They also need to be decorated with the `Port` attribute. In our case, let's set up the same three inputs we had in the C++ version of the node:

```
[Port]
public void Activate()
{
}

[Port]
public void Left(float value)
{
}

[Port]
public void Right(float value)
{
}
```

We'll come back to the implementation of `Activate` in just a second. While you can override the port name by setting optional parameters in the attribute, it's easier way to just let your function name define how the node appears in the Editor.

Adding outputs

Outputs are stored as instances of either `OutputPort` or `OutputPort<T>`, if values are required. Let's add our `Result` output now as a property on the class:

```
public OutputPort<float> Result { get; set; }
```

Implementing Activate

Let's jump back to our `Activate` input; again, we need to retrieve our two values and then fire an output. The `FlowNode` class has convenient functions for these:

```
var left = GetPortValue<float>(Left);
var right = GetPortValue<float>(Right);
var answer = left * right;

Result.Activate(answer);
```

That's it! Next time you open the Flowgraph Editor, you'll see your new **CSharpTutorial:Multiplier** node, with the exact same functionality as the C++ equivalent you implemented earlier:

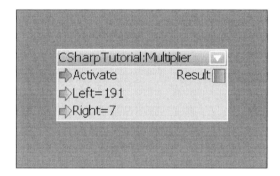

Congratulations once again, as you've taken your first step to writing game code using the .NET platform and CryENGINE!

Target entities

Adding support for target entities in CryMono is easy, simply set the `TargetsEntity` property in your `FlowNode` attribute to true:

```
[FlowNode(TargetsEntity = true)]
```

You can then obtain the entity instance via `FlowNode.TargetEntity`, assuming it was assigned inside the flowgraph containing the node.

Summary

In this chapter, we have learnt why flowgraphs can be useful to empower designers, and created our own flowgraph.

We've also investigated a selection of the existing nodes provided by CryENGINE, and then created our own nodes in two programming languages. You should now have a good understanding of the flowgraph system, and how to use it to your advantage.

In future chapters, we'll look at some of the additional things flowgraphs can achieve, including designing user interfaces, implementing material effects, creating special flownodes to represent entities in the world, and wrapping up AI functionality into convenient reusable modules.

For now, if you'd like to explore the world of flowgraphs more, why not have a go at figuring out how more of the stock nodes can be implemented? Familiarize yourself with the differences between writing C++ and C# nodes, and see which you prefer.

If you'd like to experiment with CryMono in particular, try editing your node scripts and saving them with Sandbox running; you may be pleasantly surprised to find that they're recompiled and reloaded in the background! This should help you test new node ideas without having your experimentation hindered by compile times and restarts.

3
Creating and Utilizing Custom Entities

The CryENGINE entity system provides the means for creating everything from simple physicalized objects to complex weather simulation managers.

In this chapter we will:

- Elaborate on the basic concept and implementation of the entity system
- Create our first custom entity in Lua, C#, and C++
- Learn about the game object system

Introducing the entity system

The entity system exists to spawn and manage entities in the game world. Entities are logical containers, allowing drastic changes in behavior at runtime. For example, an entity can change its model, position, and orientation at any point in the game.

Consider this; every item, weapon, vehicle, and even player that you have interacted with in the engine is an entity. The entity system is one of the most important modules present in the engine, and is dealt regularly by programmers.

The entity system, accessible via the `IEntitySystem` interface, manages all entities in the game. Entities are referenced to using the `entityId` type definition, which allows 65536 unique entities at any given time.

If an entity is marked for deletion, for example, `IEntity::Remove(bool bNow = false)`, the entity system will delete this prior to updating at the start of the next frame. If the `bNow` parameter is set to true, the entity will be removed right away.

Entity classes

Entities are simply instances of an entity class, represented by the `IEntityClass` interface. Each entity class is assigned a name that identifies it, for example, SpawnPoint.

Classes can be registered via `IEntityClassRegistry::RegisterClass`, or via `IEntityClassRegistry::RegisterStdClass` to use the default `IEntityClass` implementation.

Entities

The `IEntity` interface is used to access the entity implementation itself. The core implementation of `IEntity` is contained within `CryEntitySystem.dll`, and cannot be modified. Instead, we are able to extend entities using game object extensions (have a look at the *Game object extensions* section in this chapter) and custom entity classes.

entityId

Each entity instance is assigned a unique identifier, which persists for the duration of the game session.

EntityGUID

Besides the `entityId` parameter, entities are also given globally unique identifiers, which unlike `entityId` can persist between game sessions, in the case of saving games and more.

Game objects

When entities need extended functionality, they can utilize game objects and game object extensions. This allows for a larger set of functionality that can be shared by any entity.

Game objects allow the handling of binding entities to the network, serialization, per-frame updates, and the ability to utilize existing (or create new) game object extensions such as Inventory and AnimatedCharacter.

Typically in CryENGINE development, game objects are only necessary for more important entity implementations, such as actors. The actor system is explained more in depth in *Chapter 5, Creating Custom Actors*, along with the `IActor` game object extension.

The entity pool system

The entity pool system allows "pooling" of entities, allowing efficient control of entities that are currently being processed. This system is commonly accessed via flowgraph, and allows the disabling /enabling groups of entities at runtime based on events.

 Pools are also used for entities that need to be created and released frequently, for example, bullets.

Once an entity has been marked as handled by the pool system, it will be hidden in the game by default. Until the entity has been prepared, it will not exist in the game world. It is also ideal to free the entity once it is no longer needed.

For example, if you have a group of AI that only needs to be activated when the player reaches a predefined checkpoint trigger, this can be set up using `AreaTrigger` (and its included flownode) and the `Entity:EntityPool` flownode.

Creating a custom entity

Now that we've learned the basics of the entity system, it's time to create our first entity. For this exercise, we'll be demonstrating the ability to create an entity in Lua, C#, and finally C++.

Creating an entity using Lua

Lua entities are fairly simple to set up, and revolve around two files: the entity definition, and the script itself. To create a new Lua entity, we'll first have to create the entity definition in order to tell the engine where the script is located:

```
<Entity
  Name="MyLuaEntity"
  Script="Scripts/Entities/Others/MyLuaEntity.lua"
/>
```

Simply save this file as `MyLuaEntity.ent` in the `Game/Entities/` directory, and the engine will search for the script at `Scripts/Entities/Others/MyLuaEntity.lua`.

Now we can move on to creating the Lua script itself! To start, create the script at the path set previously and add an empty table with the same name as your entity:

```
MyLuaEntity = { }
```

When parsing the script, the first thing the engine does is search for a table with the same name as the entity, as you defined it in the .ent definition file. This main table is where we can store variables, Editor properties, and other engine information.

For example, we can add our own property by adding a string variable:

```
MyLuaEntity = {
  Properties = {
    myProperty = "",
  },
}
```

 It is possible to create property categories by adding subtables within the Properties table. This is useful for organizational purposes.

With the changes done, you should see the following screenshot when spawning an instance of your class in the Editor, via **RollupBar** present to the far right of the Editor by default:

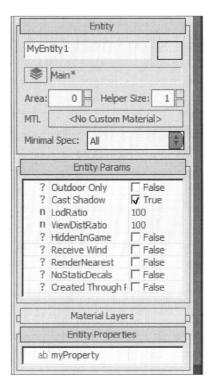

Common Lua entity callbacks

The script system provides a set of callbacks that can be utilized to trigger specific logic on entity events. For example, the OnInit function is called on the entity when it is initialized:

```
function MyEntity:OnInit()
end
```

Creating an entity in C#

The third-party extension, **CryMono** allows the creation of entities in .NET, which leads us to demonstrate the capability of creating our very own entity in C#.

To start, open the Game/Scripts/Entities directory, and create a new file called MyCSharpEntity.cs. This file will contain our entity code, and will be compiled at runtime when the engine is launched.

Now, open the script (MyCSharpEntity.cs) IDE of your choice. We'll be using Visual Studio in order to provide **IntelliSense** and code highlighting.

Once opened, let's create a basic skeleton entity. We'll need to add a reference to the CryENGINE namespace, in which the most common CryENGINE types are stored.

```
using CryEngine;

namespace CryGameCode
{
  [Entity]
  public class MyCSharpEntity : Entity
  {
  }
}
```

Now, save the file and start the Editor. Your entity should now appear in **RollupBar**, inside the **Default** category. Drag **MyEntity** into the viewport in order to spawn it:

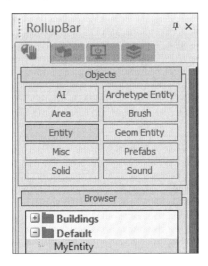

We use the entity attribute (`[Entity]`) as a way of providing additional information for the entity registration progress, for example, using the `Category` property will result in using a custom Editor category, instead of **Default**.

```
[Entity(Category = "Others")]
```

Adding Editor properties

Editor properties allow the level designer to supply parameters to the entity, perhaps to indicate the size of a trigger area, or to specify an entity's default health value.

In CryMono, this can be done by decorating supported types (have a look at the following code snippet) with the `EditorProperty` attribute. For example, if we want to add a new `string` property:

```
[EditorProperty]
public string MyProperty { get; set; }
```

Now when you start the Editor and drag **MyCSharpEntity** into the viewport, you should see **MyProperty** appear in the lower part of **RollupBar**.

The `MyProperty` string variable in C# will be automatically updated when the user edits this via the Editor. Remember that Editor properties will be saved with the level, allowing the entity to use Editor properties defined by the level designer even in pure game mode.

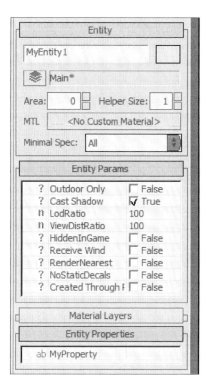

Property folders

As with Lua scripts, it is possible for CryMono entities to place Editor properties in folders for organizational purposes. In order to create folders, you can utilize the `Folder` property of the `EditorProperty` attribute as shown:

```
[EditorProperty(Folder = "MyCategory")]
```

You now know how to create entities with custom Editor properties using CryMono! This is very useful when creating simple gameplay elements for level designers to place and modify at runtime, without having to reach for the nearest programmer.

Creating an entity in C++

Creating an entity in C++ is slightly more complex than making one using Lua or C#, and can be done differently based on what the entity is required for. For this example, we'll be detailing the creation of a custom entity class by implementing IEntityClass.

Creating a custom entity class

Entity classes are represented by the IEntityClass interface, which we will derive from and register via IEntityClassRegistry::RegisterClass(IEntityClass *pClass).

To start off, let's create the header file for our entity class. Right-click on your project in Visual Studio, or any of its filters, and go to **Add** | **New Item** in the context menu. When prompted, create your header file (.h). We'll be calling CMyEntityClass.

Now, open the generated MyEntityClass.h header file, and create a new class which derives from IEntityClass:

```
#include <IEntityClass.h>

class CMyEntityClass : public IEntityClass
{
};
```

Now that we have the class set up, we'll need to implement the pure virtual methods we inherit from IEntityClass in order for our class to compile successfully.

For most of the methods, we can simply return a null pointer, zero, or an empty string. However, there are a couple of methods which we have to handle for the class to function:

- Release(): This is called when the class should be released, should simply perform "delete this;" to destroy the class
- GetName(): This should return the name of the class
- GetEditorClassInfo(): This should return the ClassInfo struct, containing Editor category, helper, and icon strings to the Editor
- SetEditorClassInfo(): This is called when something needs to update the Editor ClassInfo explained just now.

`IEntityClass` is the bare minimum for an entity class, and does not support Editor properties yet (we will cover this a bit further later).

To register an entity class, we need to call `IEntityClassRegistry::RegisterCla ss`. This has to be done prior to the `IGameFramework::CompleteInit` call in `CGameStartup`. We'll be doing it inside `GameFactory.cpp`, in the `InitGameFactory` function:

```
IEntityClassRegistry::SEntityClassDesc classDesc;

classDesc.sName = "MyEntityClass";
classDesc.editorClassInfo.sCategory = "MyCategory";

IEntitySystem *pEntitySystem = gEnv->pEntitySystem;

IEntityClassRegistry *pClassRegistry = pEntitySystem-
    >GetClassRegistry();

bool result = pClassRegistry->RegisterClass(new
    CMyEntityClass(classDesc));
```

Implementing a property handler

In order to handle Editor properties, we'll have to extend our `IEntityClass` implementation with a new implementation of `IEntityPropertyHandler`. The property handler is responsible for handling the setting, getting, and serialization of properties.

Start by creating a new header file named `MyEntityPropertyHandler.h`. Following is the bare minimum implementation of `IEntityPropertyHandler`. In order to properly support properties, you'll need to implement `SetProperty` and `GetProperty`, as well as `LoadEntityXMLProperties` (the latter being required to read property values from the `Level` XML).

Then create a new class which derives from `IEntityPropertyHandler`:

```
class CMyEntityPropertyHandler : public IEntityPropertyHandler
{
};
```

In order for the new class to compile, you'll need to implement the pure virtual methods defined in `IEntityPropertyHandler`. Methods crucial for the property handler to work properly can be seen as shown:

- `LoadEntityXMLProperties`: This is called by the Launcher when a level is being loaded, in order to read property values of entities saved by the Editor
- `GetPropertyCount`: This should return the number of properties registered with the class
- `GetPropertyInfo`: This is called to get the property information at the specified index, most importantly when the Editor gets the available properties
- `SetProperty`: This is called to set the property value for an entity
- `GetProperty`: This is called to get the property value of an entity
- `GetDefaultProperty`: This is called to retrieve the default property value at the specified index

To make use of the new property handler, create an instance of it (passing the requested properties to its constructor) and return the newly created handler inside `IEntityClass::GetPropertyHandler()`.

We now have a basic entity class implementation, which can be easily extended to support Editor properties. This implementation is very extensible, and can be used for vast amount of purposes, for example, the C# script seen later has simply automated this process, lifting the responsibility of so much code from the programmer.

Entity flownodes

In the previous chapter, we covered the flowgraph system, as well as the creation of flownodes. You may have noticed that when right-clicking inside a graph, one of the context options is **Add Selected Entity**. This functionality allows you to select an entity inside a level, and then add its entity flownode to the flowgraph.

By default, the entity flownode doesn't contain any ports, and will therefore be mostly useless as shown to the right.

However, we can easily create our own entity flownode that targets the entity we selected in all three languages.

Creating an entity flownode in Lua

By extending the entity we created in the *Creating an entity using Lua* section, we can add its very own entity flownode:

```
function MyLuaEntity:Event_OnBooleanPort()
BroadcastEvent(self, "MyBooleanOutput");
end

MyLuaEntity.FlowEvents =
{
  Inputs =
  {
    MyBooleanPort = { MyLuaEntity.Event_OnBooleanPort, "bool" },
  },
  Outputs =
  {
    MyBooleanOutput = "bool",
  },
}
```

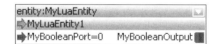

We just created an entity flownode for our `MyLuaEntity` class. If you start the Editor, spawn your entity, select it and then click on **Add Selected Entity** in your flowgraph, you should see the node appearing.

Creating an entity flownode using C#

Creating an entity flownode in C# is very simple due to being almost exactly identical in implementation as the regular flownodes. To create a new flownode for your entity, simply derive from `EntityFlowNode<T>`, where `T` is your entity class name:

```
using CryEngine.Flowgraph;

public class MyEntity : Entity { }

public class MyEntityNode : EntityFlowNode<MyEntity>
{
  [Port]
  public void Vec3Test(Vec3 input) { }

  [Port]
  public void FloatTest(float input) { }

  [Port]
  public void VoidTest()
  {
  }

  [Port]
  OutputPort<bool> BoolOutput { get; set; }
}
```

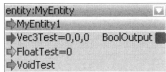

We just created an entity flownode in C#. This allows us to easily use what we learned from the previous chapter and utilize `TargetEntity` in our new node's logic.

Creating an entity flownode in C++

 This section assumes that you read *Creating a custom node in C++* section from *Chapter 2, Visual Scripting with Flowgraph*.

In short, entity flownodes are identical in implementation to regular nodes. The difference being the way the node is registered, as well as the prerequisite for the entity to support `TargetEntity` (refer to the previous chapter for more information).

Registering the entity node

We utilize same methods for registering entity nodes as before, the only difference being that the category has to be entity, and the node name has to be the same as the entity it belongs to:

```
REGISTER_FLOW_NODE("entity:MyCppEntity", CMyEntityFlowNode);
```

The final code

Finally, from what we've learned now and in the previous chapter, we can easily create our first entity flownode in C++:

```cpp
#include "stdafx.h"

#include "Nodes/G2FlowBaseNode.h"

class CMyEntityFlowNode : public CFlowBaseNode<eNCT_Instanced>
{
  enum EInput
  {
    EIP_InputPort,
  };

  enum EOutput
  {
    EOP_OutputPort
  };
```

```
public:
  CMyEntityFlowNode(SActivationInfo *pActInfo)
  {
  }

  virtual IFlowNodePtr Clone(SActivationInfo *pActInfo)
  {
    return new CMyEntityFlowNode(pActInfo);
  }

  virtual void ProcessEvent(EFlowEvent evt, SActivationInfo
    *pActInfo)
  {
  }

  virtual void GetConfiguration(SFlowNodeConfig &config)
  {
    static const SInputPortConfig inputs[] =
    {
      InputPortConfig_Void("Input", "Our first input port"),
      {0}
    };
    static const SOutputPortConfig outputs[] =
    {
      OutputPortConfig_Void("Output", "Our first output port"),
      {0}
    };

    config.pInputPorts = inputs;
    config.pOutputPorts = outputs;
    config.sDescription = _HELP("Entity flow node sample");

    config.nFlags |= EFLN_TARGET_ENTITY;
  }

  virtual void GetMemoryUsage(ICrySizer *s) const
  {
    s->Add(*this);
  }
};

REGISTER_FLOW_NODE("entity:MyCppEntity", CMyEntityFlowNode);
```

Game objects

As mentioned at the start of the chapter, game objects are used when more advanced functionality is required of an entity, for example, if an entity needs to be bound to the network.

There are two ways of implementing game objects, one being by registering the entity directly via `IGameObjectSystem::RegisterExtension` (and thereby having the game object automatically created on entity spawn), and the other is by utilizing the `IGameObjectSystem::CreateGameObjectForEntity` method to create a game object for an entity at runtime.

Game object extensions

It is possible to extend game objects by creating extensions, allowing the developer to hook into a number of entity and game object callbacks. This is, for example, how actors are implemented by default, something we'll be covering in *Chapter 5*, *Creating Custom Actors*.

We will be creating our game object extension in C++. The CryMono entity we created earlier in the chapter was made possible by a custom game object extension contained in `CryMono.dll`, and it is currently not possible to create further extensions via C# or Lua.

Creating a game object extension in C++

CryENGINE provides a helper class template for creating a game object extension, called `CGameObjectExtensionHelper`. This helper class is used to avoid duplicating common code that is necessary for most game object extensions, for example, basic RMI functionality (we'll cover them in *Chapter 8*, *Multiplayer and Networking*).

To properly implement `IGameObjectExtension`, simply derive from the `CGameObjectExtensionHelper` template, specifying the first template argument as the class you're writing (in our case, `CMyEntityExtension`) and the second as `IGameObjectExtension` you're looking to derive from.

Normally, the second argument is `IGameObjectExtension`, but it can be different for specific implementations such as `IActor` (which in turn derives from `IGameObjectExtension`).

```
class CMyGameObjectExtension
  : public CGameObjectExtensionHelper<CMyGameObjectExtension,
    IGameObjectExtension>
  {

  };
```

Now that you've derived from `IGameObjectExtension`, you'll need to implement all its pure virtual methods to spare yourself from a bunch of unresolved externals. Most can be overridden with empty methods that return nothing or false, while more important ones have been listed as shown:

- Init: This is called to initialize the extension. Simply perform `SetGameObject(pGameObject);` and then return true.

- `NetSerialize`: This is called to serialize things over the network. This will be covered in *Chapter 8, Multiplayer and Networking*, but for now, it will simply return true.

You'll also need to implement `IGameObjectExtensionCreatorBase` in a new class that will serve as an extension factory for your entity. When the extension is about to be activated, our factory's `Create()` method will be called in order to obtain the new extension instance:

```
struct SMyGameObjectExtensionCreator
  : public IGameObjectExtensionCreatorBase
{
  virtual IGameObjectExtension *Create() { return new
    CMyGameObjectExtension(); }

  virtual void GetGameObjectExtensionRMIData(void **ppRMI,
    size_t *nCount) { return
    CMyGameObjectExtension::GetGameObjectExtensionRMIData
      (ppRMI, nCount); }
};
```

Now that you've created both your game object extension implementation, as well as the game object creator, simply register the extension:

```
static SMyGameObjectExtensionCreator creator;
gEnv->pGameFramework->GetIGameObjectSystem()-
    >RegisterExtension("MyGameObjectExtension", &creator,
      myEntityClassDesc);
```

By passing the entity class description to `IGameObjectSystem::R egisterExtension`, you're telling it to create a dummy entity class for you. If you have already done so, simply pass the last parameter `pEntityCls` as `NULL` to make it use the class you registered before.

Activating our extension

In order to activate your game object extension, you'll need to call `IGameObject::ActivateExtension` after the entity is spawned. One way to do this is using the entity system sink, `IEntitySystemSink`, and listening to the `OnSpawn` events.

We've now registered our own game object extension. When the entity is spawned, our entity system sink's `OnSpawn` method will be called, allowing us to create an instance of our game object extension.

Summary

In this chapter, we have learned how the core entity system is implemented and exposed and created our own custom entity.

You should now be aware of the process of creating accompanying flownodes for your entities, and be aware of the working knowledge surrounding game objects and their extensions.

We'll be covering existing game object extensions and entity implementations in latter chapters, for example, by creating our very own actor and implementing basic AI.

If you want to get more familiar with the entity system, why not try and create a slightly more complex entity on your own?

In the next chapter, we'll be covering the game rules system.

4
Game Rules

Actors and entities are integral parts of the game, but game rules are what tie them together. The game rules system manages all initial player events, such as OnConnect, OnDisconnect, and OnEnteredGame.

Using the game rules system, we can create custom game flow to control and tie our gameplay mechanics together.

In this chapter we will:

- Learn the basic concept of a game mode
- Create our IGameRules implementation in C++
- Write game rules scripts in Lua and C#

Introduction to game rules

When thinking of a game, we typically direct our thoughts to game mechanics such as the handling of deaths and end game conditions. Based on what we've learned in the previous chapters, we can't really accomplish this due to every entity and actor not affecting a grander scheme.

Game rules do exactly what the name implies; control the rules of the game. A rule can be simple, like a rule for what happens when one actor shoots the other, or more complex, for example, start and end rounds.

The CryENGINE game rules implementation revolves around two very similar sounding types that are still quite different:

- **Game rules**: This implementation is done via the IGameRules interface in C++, and it handles callbacks such as OnClientConnect and OnClientDisconnect.

- **Game mode**: This is reliant on the game rules implementation, but extends it with game conditions such as actor spawning and kill conditions. For example, we could have two game modes; SinglePlayer and DeathMatch, both which rely on the default behavior provided by the IGameRules implementation, but each adding additional functionality, such as support for multiple players.

IGameRules interface – game rules

At the end of *Chapter 3, Creating and Utilizing Custom Entities*, we learned about game object extensions. We'll be using that knowledge in this chapter to implement IGameRules, a game object extension used to initialize the game context and tie gameplay mechanics together.

> Always keep in mind that the currently active game mode is an entity. This can sometimes be abused by requesting entity events. For example, a common hack in the Crytek game, Crysis, revolved around sending a bullet or kill event on the game mode. This essentially "killed" the game rules entity and resulted in a hard server crash.

The IGameRules implementation is commonly responsible for the most basic behavior of your game modes, and forwards everything else to its C# or Lua script.

Scripting – game modes

After registering our IGameRules implementation, we'll need to register a game mode that utilizes it. This is done using the IGameRulesSystem::RegisterGameRul es function (commonly done inside IGame::Init).

```
pGameRulesSystem->RegisterGameRules("MyGameMode", "GameRules");
```

After having processed the previous snippet, the game rules system will be aware of our game mode. When the sv_gamerules console variable is changed to MyGameMode, the system will create a new entity and activate its game object extension called GameRules (registered in the previous section).

> The console variable sv_gamerules is set to the value of sv_ gamerulesdefault on CryENGINE startup, unless running on a dedicated server.

At this point, the game will automatically search for a Lua script named after your game mode in Scripts/GameRules/. For the previous snippet, it would find and load Scripts/GameRules/MyGameMode.lua.

By using scripts, the game rules implementation can forward game events (such as new player connections) to Lua or C#, allowing each game mode to specialize behavior depending on its internal logic.

Loading a level

When a level is loaded using the map console command, the game framework searches for the level inside `Game/Levels`.

By using `IGameRulesSystem::AddGameRulesLevelLocation`, we can add subdirectories within `Game/Levels` which will be searched when looking for a new level. For example:

```
gEnv->pGameFramework->GetIGameRulesSystem()->AddGameRulesLevelLocation
("MyGameMode", "MGM_Levels");
```

When loading a level with `sv_gamerules` set to `MyGameMode`, the game framework will now search in the `Levels/MGM_Levels/` directory for the level directory.

This allows game mode specific levels to be moved to subdirectories within the `Game/Levels` directory, making it much easier to sort levels by game mode.

Implementing the game rules interface

Now that we know the basic workings of the game rules system, we can give creating a custom `IGameRules` implementation a shot.

 Before we start, consider whether you actually need a custom `IGameRules` implementation for your game. The default GameDLL that ships with `CGameRules`, is an `IGameRules` implementation specialized for **First-Person Shooters** (**FPS**). If your game premise is similar to a FPS, or if you can reuse existing functionality that might be preferrable to writing an implementation from scratch.

To start, we'll need to create two new files; `GameRules.cpp` and `GameRules.h`. When you're done, open `GameRules.h` and create a new class. We'll be naming ours as `CGameRules`.

After the class is in place, we have to derive from IGameRules. As we mentioned before, game rules are handled as game object extensions. We'll therefore have to use the CGameObjectExtensionHelper template class:

```
class CGameRules
  : public CGameObjectExtensionHelper<CGameRules, IGameRules>
  {

  };
```

The third and optional CGameObjectExtensionHelper parameter defines how many RMIs this game object support. We'll cover it further in *Chapter 8, Multiplayer and Networking*.

With the class present, we can start implementing all the pure virtual methods defined in the IGameRules and IGameObjectExtension structs. As with entities, we can implement dummies that return either nothing, nullptr, zero, false or an empty string. The methods that need to be handled separately are as follows:

Function name	Description
IGameObjectExtension::Init	Called to initialize the game object extension. Should call IGameRulesSystem::SetCurrentGameRules(this)
IGameRules::OnClientConnect	Called on the server when a new client connects, has to create a new actor using IActorSystem::CreateActor
IGameRules::OnClientDisconnect	Called on the server when a client disconnects, has to contain a call to IActorSystem::RemoveActor
IGameObjectExtension::Release / Destructor	The Release function should delete the extension instance and call IGameRulesSystem::SetCurrentGameRules(nullptr) via its the destructor

Registering the game object extension

When you're done, register the game rules implementation by using the REGISTER_FACTORY macro.

Game object extensions have to be registered early in the game initialization process, and therefore most commonly done in the IGame::Init function (via GameFactory.cpp in the default GameDLL):

```
REGISTER_FACTORY(pFramework, "GameRules", CGameRules, false);
```

Creating custom game modes

To get started, we'll need to register our first game mode.

 Note the difference between the `IGameRules` implementation, and the game mode itself. The game mode is dependent on the `IGameRules` implementation, and is registered separately.

To register custom game modes, CryENGINE exposes the `IGameRulesSystem::Reg isterGameRules` function:

```
gEnv->pGameFramework->GetIGameRulesSystem()-
    >RegisterGameRules("MyGameMode", "GameRules");
```

The previous code will create a game mode called `MyGameMode`, which depends on the `GameRules` game object extension we registered earlier.

When a map is loaded with `sv_gamerules` set to `MyGameMode`, the game rules entity will be created and assigned the name `MyGameMode`. After spawning, the `IGameRules` extension we created earlier will be constructed.

 If you are simply creating a copy or subclass of an existing game mode, for example, the default `DeathMatch.lua` script that derives from `SinglePlayer.lua`, you'll need to register the `DeathMatch` game mode separately.

Scripting

Game modes are typically heavily scripting-oriented, with game flow such as spawning, killing, and reviving being delegated to a secondary language such as Lua or C#.

Lua scripting

As Lua scripts are integrated into the CryENGINE, we don't need to do any additional loading for it to work. To access your script table (based on the Lua file named the same as your game mode in `Game/Scripts/GameRules`):

```
m_script = GetEntity()->GetScriptTable();
```

Invoking methods

To invoke methods on your script table, see the IScriptSystem BeginCall and EndCall functions:

```
IScriptSystem *pScriptSystem = gEnv->pScriptSystem;

pScriptSystem->BeginCall(m_script, "MyMethod");
pScriptSystem->EndCall();
```

When executing the previous code, we'll be able to execute Lua code in a function named MyMethod contained inside our game mode's script table. An example of the table can be seen as follows:

```
MyGameMode = { }

function MyGameMode:MyMethod()
end
```

Invoking methods with parameters

To provide your Lua method with parameters, use IScriptSystem::PushFuncParam between the beginning and end of your script call:

```
pScriptSystem->BeginCall(m_script, name);
pScriptSystem->PushFuncParam("myStringParameter");
pScriptSystem->EndCall();
```

 IScriptSystem::PushFuncParam is a template function that attempts to create a ScriptAnyValue object with the provided value. If the default ScriptAnyValue constructors don't support your type, a compiler error will appear.

Congratulations, you have now called a Lua function with a string parameter:

```
function MyGameMode:MyMethod(stringParam)
end
```

Getting values returned from Lua

You can also get return values from Lua functions by passing an additional parameter to IScriptSystem::EndCall.

```
int result = 0;
pScriptSystem->EndCall(&result);
CryLog("MyMethod returned %i!", result);
```

Getting table values

Sometimes it might be necessary to get values directly from Lua tables, this can be done using `IScriptTable::GetValue`:

```
bool bValue = false;
m_script->GetValue("bMyBool", &bValue);
```

The previous code will search for a variable called `bMyBool` in the script, and if successful, set its value to the native `bValue` variable.

CryMono scripting

To create an instance of a CryMono script in your `IGameObjectExtension::Init` implementation, see `IMonoScriptSystem::InstantiateScript`:

```
IMonoObjaect *pScript = GetMonoScriptSystem()-
  >InstantiateScript(GetEntity()->GetClass()->GetName(),
    eScriptFlag_GameRules);
```

This code will find a CryMono class with the current game mode's name, and return a new instance of it.

 There is no need to use both Lua and CryMono game rules scripts simultaneously. Decide which is best for your use case.

Calling methods

Now that you have your class instance, you can invoke one of its functions using the `IMonoObject::CallMethod` helper:

```
m_pScript->CallMethod("OnClientConnect", channelId, isReset,
  playerName)
```

This code will search for a method named `OnClientConnect` with matching arguments, and invoke it:

```
public bool OnClientConnect(int channelId, bool isReset = false,
  string playerName = "")
{
}
```

Return values

`IMonoObject::CallMethod` returns a `mono::object` type by default, which represents a boxed managed object. To get the native value, we'll have to unbox it:

```
mono::object result = m_pScript->CallMethod("OnClientConnect",
  channelId, isReset, playerName);

IMonoObject *pResult = *result;
bool result = pResult->Unbox<bool>();
```

Properties

To get the value of a property in your managed object, have a look at
`IMonoObject::GetPropertyValue`:

```
mono::object propertyValue = m_pScript-
  >GetPropertyValue("MyFloatProperty");

if(propertyValue)
{
  IMonoObject *pObject = *propertyValue;

  float value = pObject->Unbox<float>();
}
```

It is also possible to set property values directly:

```
float myValue = 5.5f;

mono::object boxedValue = GetMonoScriptSystem()-
  >GetActiveDomain()->BoxAnyValue(MonoAnyValue(myValue));

m_pScript->SetPropertyValue("MyFloatProperty", boxedValue);
```

Fields

It is also possible to get and set the values of fields in the same way you would
with properties, but using the `IMonoObject` methods, `GetFieldValue` and
`SetFieldValue`.

Creating a basic game mode in C#

Now that we have the basic knowledge required to create a mini-game, why not
do so? To start off, we'll aim towards creating a very basic system for spawning
actors and entities.

Defining our intention

To start, let's clarify exactly what we want to do:

1. Spawn our actor.

2. Assign our actor to one of the two possible teams.

3. Check when an actor enters the opposite team's `Headquarters` entity, and end it.

Creating the actor

The first thing we need to do is spawn our actor, which can't be done before we have one. To do this, we'll need to create a `MyActor.cs` file somewhere in the `Game/Scripts` directory and then add the following code:

```
public class MyActor : Actor
{
}
```

This code snippet is the bare minimum required for an actor to be registered.

We should also update our actor's view, to make sure the player sees something when entering the game.

```
protected override void UpdateView(ref ViewParams viewParams)
{
  var fov = MathHelpers.DegreesToRadians(60);

  viewParams.FieldOfView = fov;
  viewParams.Position = Position;
  viewParams.Rotation = Rotation;
}
```

The previous code will simply set the camera to use the player entities' position and rotation, with a field of view of 60.

 To learn more about creating actors and views, refer to *Chapter 5, Creating Custom Actors*.

Now that we have our actor, we can move on to creating the game mode:

```
public class ReachTheHeadquarters : CryEngine.GameRules
{

}
```

As with all CryMono types found in the `Game/Scripts/` directory, our game mode will be automatically registered on CryENGINE startup, shortly after the call to `IGameFramework::Init`.

Before moving on to creating game-specific logic, we'll have to make sure our actor is created when the actor connects. To do so, we implement an `OnClientConnect` method:

```
public bool OnClientConnect(int channelId, bool isReset = false,
  string playerName = "Dude")
{
  // Only the server can create actors.
  if (!Game.IsServer)
    return false;

  var actor = Actor.Create<MyActor>(channelId, playerName);
  if (actor == null)
  {
    Debug.LogWarning("Failed to create the player.");
    return false;
  }

  return true;
}
```

However, as script functions aren't automated, we'll need to modify our `IGameRules` implementation's `OnClientConnect` method to make sure we receive this callback in C#:

```
bool CGameRules::OnClientConnect(int channelId, bool isReset)
{
const char *playerName;
if (gEnv->bServer && gEnv->bMultiplayer)
{
  if (INetChannel *pNetChannel = gEnv->pGameFramework-
    >GetNetChannel(channelId))
    playerName = pNetChannel->GetNickname();
}
  else
    playerName = "Dude";

return m_pScript->CallMethod("OnClientConnect", channelId,
    isReset, playerName) != 0;
}
```

Now, when a new player connects to the server, our `IGameRules` implementation will call `ReachTheHeadquarters.OnClientConnect`, which in turn creates a new actor of type `MyActor`.

 Keep in mind that the game mode's `OnClientConnect` is called very early, right at the point when a new client is connecting to the server. If an actor has not been created for the specified `channelId` after `OnClientConnect` exits, the game will throw a fatal error.

Spawning the actor

The actor will now be created when the client connects, but what about actually repositioning the actor to a **SpawnPoint**? To start, create a new `SpawnPoint.cs` file somewhere in the `Scripts` directory:

```
[Entity(Category = "Others", EditorHelper =
  "Editor/Objects/spawnpointhelper.cgf")]
public class SpawnPoint : Entity
{
  public void Spawn(EntityBase otherEntity)
  {
    otherEntity.Position = this.Position;
    otherEntity.Rotation = this.Rotation;
  }
}
```

This entity should now appear in **RollupBar** after you restart the Editor. We'll be calling the `spawnPoint.Spawn` function to spawn our actor.

To start, we'll need to open our `ReachTheHeadquarters` class and add a new `OnClientEnteredGame` function:

```
public void OnClientEnteredGame(int channelId, EntityId
  playerId, bool reset)
{
  var player = Actor.Get<MyActor>(channelId);
  if (player == null)
  {
    Debug.LogWarning("Failed to get player");
    return;
  }
```

```
        var random = new Random();

    // Get all spawned entities off type SpawnPoint
        var spawnPoints = Entity.GetByClass<SpawnPoint>();

    // Get a random spawpoint
        var spawnPoint =
          spawnPoints.ElementAt(random.Next(spawnPoints.Count()));
        if(spawnPoint != null)
        {
         // Found one! Spawn the player here.
          spawnPoint.Spawn(player);
        }
    }
```

This function will be called when the client enters the game. In Launcher mode this typically happens when the player has finished loading, whereas in Editor it is called when the player switches into **pure game mode** following *Ctrl + G*.

At its current state, we'll first get the MyActor instance of our player, and then spawn at a randomly selected SpawnPoint.

Don't forget to call your script's OnClientEnteredGame function from your IGameRules implementation!

Handling disconnections

We'll also have to make sure the actor is removed when the player disconnects:

```
    public override void OnClientDisconnect(int channelId)
    {
      Actor.Remove(channelId);
    }
```

Don't forget to call the OnClientConnect function from your IGameRules implementation!

Failure to remove the player after disconnection will result in the actor persisting in the game world, and more severe issues can appear due to the associated player no longer having a connection to the server.

Assigning the player to a team

Now that players can connect and spawn, let's implement a basic teams system to keep track of which team each player belongs to.

First off, let's add a new `Teams` property to our game mode:

```
public virtual IEnumerable<string> Teams
{
  get
  {
    return new string[] { "Red", "Blue" };
  }
}
```

This code simply determines which teams our game mode allows for, in our case `Red` and `Blue`.

Now, let's also add a new property to our `MyActor` class, to determine which team the actor belongs to:

```
public string Team { get; set; }
```

Great! However, we'll also need to add the same snippet to the `SpawnPoint` entity to avoid spawning players of the same team next to each other.

Once you have done this, open the `ReachTheHeadquarters` game mode class and navigate to the `OnClientEnteredGame` function we created earlier. What we want to do is expand the `SpawnPoint` selection to only use ones belonging to the player's team.

Have a look at the following snippet:

```
// Get all spawned entities of type SpawnPoint
   var spawnPoints = Entity.GetByClass<SpawnPoint>();
```

Now, replace this snippet with the following one:

```
// Get all spawned entities of type SpawnPoint belonging to the
   players team
   var spawnPoints = Entity.GetByClass<SpawnPoint>().Where(x =>
     x.Team == player.Team);
```

This will automatically remove all SpawnPoints in which the `Team` property is not equal to that of the player.

But wait, we also have to assign the player to a team! To do so, add the following before getting the SpawnPoints:

```
player.Team = Teams.ElementAt(random.Next(Teams.Count()));
```

When a player enters the game, we'll select a random team to assign them to. If you want, why not expand this to make sure teams are always balanced? For example, don't allow a new player to join team Red if it already has two more players than Blue.

 Before moving on, feel free to play around with the current setup. You should be able to spawn in game!

Implementing Headquarters

Finally, let's move on to creating our end game condition; Headquarters. In simple terms, each team will have one `Headquarters` entity, and when a player enters the headquarters of the opposite team, that player's team wins the game.

Adding the end game event

Before creating the `Headquarters` entity, let's add a new `EndGame` function to our `ReachTheHeadquarters` class:

```
public void EndGame(string winningTeam)
{
  Debug.LogAlways("{0} won the game!", winningTeam);
}
```

We'll call this from the `Headquarters` entity, in order to notify the game mode that the game should be ended.

Creating the Headquarters entity

Now, we need to create our `Headquarters` entity (see the following code snippet). The entity will be placed in each level via Sandbox, once per team. We'll expose three Editor properties; `Team`, `Minimum`, and `Maximum`:

- `Team`: This determines which team the `Headquarters` instance belongs to, in our case either Blue or Red
- `Minimum`: This specifies the minimum size of the trigger area

- `Maximum`: This specifies the maximum size of the trigger area

```
public class Headquarters : Entity
{
  public override void OnSpawn()
  {
    TriggerBounds = new BoundingBox(Minimum, Maximum);
  }

  protected override void OnEnterArea(EntityId entityId, int areaId,
EntityId areaEntityId)
  {
  }

  [EditorProperty]
  public string Team { get; set; }

  [EditorProperty]
  public Vec3 Minimum { get; set; }

  [EditorProperty]
  public Vec3 Maximum { get; set; }
}
```

Great! Now we just have to expand the `OnEnterArea` method to notify our game mode when the game should end:

```
protected override void OnEnterArea(EntityId entityId, int
  areaId, EntityId areaEntityId)
{
  var actor = Actor.Get<MyActor>(entityId);
  if (actor == null)
    return;

  if (actor.Team != Team)
  {
    var gameMode = CryEngine.GameRules.Current;
    var rthGameRules = gameMode as ReachTheHeadquarters;

    if (rthGameRules != null)
      rthGameRules.EndGame(actor.Team);
  }
}
```

The `Headquarters` entity will now notify the game mode when an entity of the opposite team enters it.

Detour – trigger bounds and entity areas

Entities can receive area callbacks by registering an area. This can be done by linking the entity to a shape entity or by creating a trigger proxy manually. In C# you can create a proxy manually by setting the `EntityBase.TriggerBounds` property as we have done in the previous code snippet.

When an entity is positioned inside or close to the area, it will start receiving events on that entity. This allows specific entities to be created that can track when and where players enter specific areas, to trigger specialized gameplay logic.

See the following table for a list of available area callbacks, receivable via entity events in C++ and virtual functions in the C# `Entity` class:

Callback name	Description
OnEnterArea	Called when an entity has entered the area linked to this entity
OnLeaveArea	Triggered when an entity present inside the area linked to this entity has left
OnEnterNearArea	Triggers when an entity moves near the area linked to this entity
OnMoveNearArea	Called when an entity moves near the area linked to this entity
OnLeaveNearArea	Called when an entity leaves the area near to the area linked to this entity
OnMoveInsideArea	Triggered when an entity is repositioned inside the area linked to this entity

Populating the level

The basic sample is now complete, but requires some tweaks to get it working! First, we'll need to create a new level and place `Headquarters` for each team.

To start, open the Sandbox Editor and create a new level by navigating to **File** | **New**:

This brings up the **New Level** dialog, in which we can set the level name and terrain settings.

After clicking on **OK**, your level will be created and then loaded. Once done, it's time to start adding the necessary gameplay elements to our level!

To start, open **RollupBar** and spawn the **Headquarters** entity by dragging it into the viewport:

Once spawned, we have to set the Editor properties we created in the **Headquarters** class.

Set **Team** to **Red** and **Maximum** to **10,10,10**. This informs the class of which team Headquarters belongs to, and the maximum size of the area which we'll be querying to detect whether another player has entered it.

Once you have done this, spawn another **Headquarters** entity (or copy the existing one) and follow the same process, except this time set the **Team** property to **Blue**.

Now, we just have to spawn one SpawnPoint entity per team and we're ready to go! Open **RollupBar** again and go to **Others | SpawnPoint**:

Now, drag the entity onto the viewport to spawn it in the same way you did to spawn **Headquarters**. Once spawned, set the **Team** property to **Red** and then repeat the process for the Blue team:

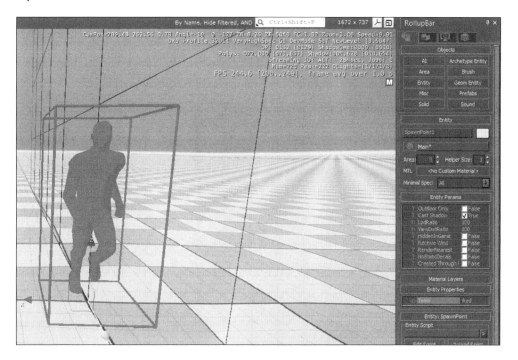

Done! You should now be able to enter the game using *Ctrl + G* or by navigating to **Game | Switch to Game**. However, as we haven't added any type of player movement, the players won't be able to navigate towards the enemy headquarters to end the game.

To learn how to handle player input and movement, refer to the next chapter, *Chapter 5, Creating Custom Actors*.

Summary

In this chapter, we have learned the basic behavior of the game rules system, and created our own `IGameRules` implementation.

After having registered your own game mode, and created the `Headquarters` sample in C#, you should have a good understanding of the game rules system.

We've created our first game mode, and can now move onto the next chapter. Keep in mind the purpose of game rules in future chapters, so you can tie together all the game mechanics that need to be created in a game.

Not satisfied with game rules yet? Why not try and create a basic rule-set for your game in a scripting language of your choice, or perhaps extend the sample we created previously. In the next chapter, we will see how to create custom actors.

5
Creating Custom Actors

Using the CryENGINE actor system, we can create players or AI-controlled entities with custom behaviors to populate our game world.

In this chapter we will cover the following topics:

- Learning the purpose of actors and the core idea behind implementing them
- Creating a custom actor in C++ and C#
- Creating our first player camera handler
- Implementing basic player movement

Introducing the actor system

We learned what game object extensions were, and how to use them, in *Chapter 3, Creating and Utilizing Custom Entities*. We'll be building upon this knowledge to create a custom actor in C++ and C#.

Actors are represented by the `IActor` struct, and they are the game object extensions in the core. This means that each actor has a backing entity, and a game object to handle networking and the `IActor` extension.

Actors are handled by the `IActorSystem` interface, which manages the creation, removal, and registration of each actor.

Channel identifiers

In networked contexts, each player is assigned a channel ID and an index for the Net Nub, which we'll cover further in *Chapter 8, Multiplayer and Networking*.

Actor spawning

Player actors should be spawned when a client connects to the game, inside IGameRules::OnClientConnect. To spawn an actor, use IActorSystem::CreateActor as shown:

```
IActorSystem *pAS = gEnv->pGameFramework->GetIActorSystem();

pAS ->CreateActor(channelId, "MyPlayerName", "MyCppActor", Vec3(0,
    0, 0), Quat(IDENTITY), Vec3(1, 1, 1));
```

Note that the previous code only applies to player-controlled actors. Non-player actors can be created at any time.

Removing actors

To make sure that the player actor is properly removed when the client disconnects, we'll need to manually remove it via the IGameRules::OnClientDisconnect callback:

```
pActorSystem->RemoveActor(myActorEntityId);
```

Forgetting to remove the players actor after they have disconnected is likely to result in crashes or severe artifacts.

The view system

In order to facilitate the need for a way to handle views for players and other camera sources, CryENGINE provides the view system, accessible via the IViewSystem interface.

The view system is based around having any number of views, represented by the IView interface, each with the ability to update the position, orientation, and configuration (such as the field of view) of the view camera.

Keep in mind that only one view can be active at any one point in time.

New views can be created using the IViewSystem::CreateView method as shown:

```
IViewSystem *pViewSystem = gEnv->pGame->GetIGameFramework()-
    >GetIViewSystem();

IView *pNewView = pViewSystem->CreateView();
```

We can then set the active view using the `IViewSystem::SetActiveView` function:

```
pViewSystem_>SetActiveView(pNewView);
```

Once activated, the view will update the system camera for each frame. To modify the parameters of your view, we can call `IView::SetCurrentParams`. For example, to change the position, use the following code snippet:

```
SViewParams viewParams = *GetCurrentParams();
viewParams.position = Vec3(0, 0, 10);
SetCurrentParams(viewParams);
```

The current position of the view will now be (0, 0, 10).

Linking views to game objects

Each view can also link itself to a game object, allowing its game object extensions to subscribe to `UpdateView` and `PostUpdateView` functions.

These functions allow the position, orientation, and configuration of the assigned view of each frame, to be easily updated. For example, this is used for actors in order to provide an accessible way of creating custom camera handling for each player.

For more information on camera handling, see the *Camera handling* section later in this chapter.

Creating custom actors

Now that we know how the actor system works, we can move on to creating our first actor in C# and C++.

 By default, it is not possible to create actors purely using the Lua scripts. Typically, the actor is created in C++ and handles custom callbacks to a Lua script contained in the `Game/Scripts/Entities/Actors` folder.

Creating actors in C#

Using CryMono, we can create custom actors entirely in C#. To do so, we can derive from the `Actor` class as shown:

```
public class MyActor : Actor
{
}
```

The previous code is the bare minimum for creating an actor in CryMono. You can then navigate to your game rules implementation and spawn the actor once the client connects via the `Actor.Create` static method.

The CryMono class hierarchy

If you find yourself confused by the various CryMono/C# classes, see the following inheritance graph:

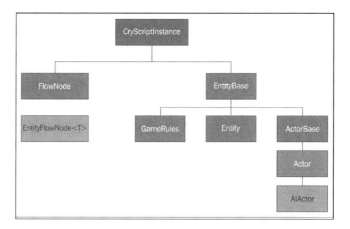

Note that while querying entities using `Entity.Get` (or actors via `Actor.Get`), you'll get an object of type `EntityBase` or `ActorBase`. This is because the native entities and actors exist outside the managed systems, and a limited representation is returned when queried for.

Using native and CryMono actors alongside each other

If you prefer creating your actor on your own in C++, you can still refer to it in CryMono code by using the `NativeActor` class. To do this, simply create a new class in C# with the name you registered your `IActor` implementation with, and derive from `NativeActor` as shown:

C++ actor registration

Actor registration is done using a registration factory. This process can be automated using the REGISTER_FACTORY macro as shown:

```
REGISTER_FACTORY(pFramework, "Player", CPlayer, false);
```

C# declaration

Declaring a native-based actor in C# is very easy, and only requires deriving from the CryEngine.NativeActor class as shown in the following code:

```
public class Player : NativeActor
{
}
```

This allows C# code to still be used, but keeps the majority of your code in your C++ IActor implementation.

> CryEngine.NativeActor derives directly from CryEngine.ActorBase, and, therefore, does not contain common CryEngine.Actor callbacks such as OnEditorReset. To get this additional functionality, you'll need to create it in your IActor implementation.

Creating actors in C++

To create an actor in C++, we rely on the IActor interface. As actors are game object extensions in the core, we can't simply derive from IActor, but have to use the CGameObjectExtensionHelper template as shown in the following code:

```
class CMyCppActor
  : public CGameObjectExtensionHelper<CMyCppActor, IActor>
{
};
```

> The third CGameObjectExtensionHelper parameter defines the maximum number of RMI's (remote machine invocations) this game object supports. We'll cover it further in *Chapter 8, Multiplayer and Networking*.

Now that we have the class, we'll need to implement the pure virtual methods defined in the IActor struct.

Note that `IActor` derives from `IGameObjectExtension`, which means that we'll also need to implement its pure virtual methods. For information on this, please see the *Implementing the game rules interface* section of *Chapter 4, Game Rules*.

For most of the `IActor` methods, we can implement dummies that either return nothing, or a dummy value such as nullptr, zero, or an empty string. The exceptions are listed in the following table:

Function name	Description
`IGameObjectExtension::Init`	Called to initialize the game object extension. Should call `IGameObjectExtension::SetGameObject` and `IActorSystem::AddActor`.
Class destructor	Should always invoke `IActorSystem::RemoveActor`.
`IActor::IsPlayer`	Used to determine whether the actor is controlled by a human player. We can simply return `GetChannelId() != 0` here, as the channel identifier is only non-zero for players.
`IActor::GetActorClassName`	Called to get the name of the actor class, for example, in our case `CMyCppActor`.
`IActor::GetEntityClassName`	Helper function to get the name of the entity class. We can simply return `GetEntity()->GetClass()->GetName()`.

When you've resolved the pure virtual functions, move on to the next section to register your actor. After having done so, you can create your actor for connecting players in `IGameRules::OnClientConnect`.

Registering actors

To register an actor with the game framework (contained in `CryAction.dll`), we can use the same setup as we used while registering our C++ game rules implementation in `GameFactory.cpp`:

```
REGISTER_FACTORY(pFramework, "MyCppActor", CMyCppActor, false);
```

After the previous code has been executed, you'll be able to spawn your actor via the `IActorSystem::CreateActor` function.

Camera handling

Player-controlled actors manage the viewport camera within the `IActor::UpdateView(SViewParams &viewParams)` and `IActor::PostUpdateView (SViewParams &viewParams)` functions.

The `SViewParams` struct is used to define camera properties such as position, rotation, and field of view. By modifying the `viewParams` reference inside the `UpdateView` method, we can move our camera to the position we require for our game.

 CryMono actors receive and handle the `UpdateView(ref ViewParams viewParams)` and `PostUpdateView(ref ViewParams viewParams)` events in the same way C++ actors do.

Implementing IGameObjectView

In order to get view events, we'll need to implement and register a game object view. To do so, start by deriving from `IGameObjectView`, and implement the following two pure virtuals it includes:

- `UpdateView`: This is called to update the view position, rotation, and field of view

- `PostUpdateView`: This is called after having updated the view

After implementing the game object view, we'll need to make sure we capture it when our actor extension is initialized (in Init):

```
if(!GetGameObject()->CaptureView(this))
    return false;
```

Your actor should now receive view update callbacks, which can be utilized to move the viewport camera. Don't forget to release the view in your destructor:

```
GetGameObject()->ReleaseView(this);
```

Creating a top-down camera

To show how create a custom camera, we'll be expanding the sample we created in the previous chapter to add a custom top-down view camera. The idea is simply to view the character from the top, and follow its movements from a distance.

To start, open your C# actor's `UpdateView` method, or implement it in your `.cs` source file.

View rotation

To make the view face the top of the player, we'll be using the second column of the player's rotation in order to get the up direction.

 Quaternions represent the player's rotation in a manner that allows for easy interpolation and avoiding gimbal locks. You can obtain three columns representing directions of each quaternion: 0 (right), 1 (forward), and 2 (up). This is very useful, for example, to get a vector facing the player's forward direction.

Unless you've made any changes to your actors `UpdateView` function since the last function, it should look similar to the following code snippet:

```
protected override void UpdateView(ref ViewParams viewParams)
{
  var fov = MathHelpers.DegreesToRadians(60);

  viewParams.FieldOfView = fov;
  viewParams.Position = Position;
  viewParams.Rotation = Rotation
}
```

This simply puts the view camera in the exactly same position as the player, with the same orientation. The first change we'll have to do is move the camera up a bit.

To do so, we'll simply append the second column of the player's rotation to its position, and placing the camera at the same x and y position as the player, but slightly above it:

```
var playerRotation = Rotation;

float distanceFromPlayer = 5;
var upDir = playerRotation.Column2;

viewParams.Position = Position + upDir * distanceFromPlayer;
```

Feel free to go in-game and check it out. When you're ready, we also have to change the view rotation to look straight down:

```
// Face straight down
var angles = new Vec3(MathHelpers.DegreesToRadians(-90), 0, 0);

//Convert to Quaternion
viewParams.Rotation = Quat.CreateRotationXYZ(angles);
```

Done! Our camera should now be facing straight down.

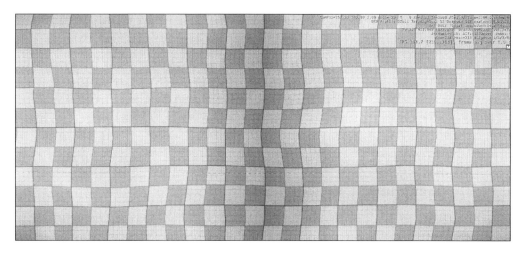

This is roughly what you should be seeing with the new camera.

Note the lack of a player character in view. This is because we haven't loaded an object into the player entity. We can quickly resolve this by calling `EntityBase.LoadObject` in the `OnSpawn` function:

```
public override void OnSpawn()
{
  // Load object
  LoadObject("Objects/default/primitive_cube.cgf");

  // Physicalize to weigh 50KG
  var physicalizationParams = new
    PhysicalizationParams(PhysicalizationType.Rigid);
  physicalizationParams.mass = 50;
  Physicalize(physicalizationParams);
}
```

You should now be able to see a cube representing the player character in the scene. Note that it is also physicalized, allowing it to push or get pushed by other physicalized objects.

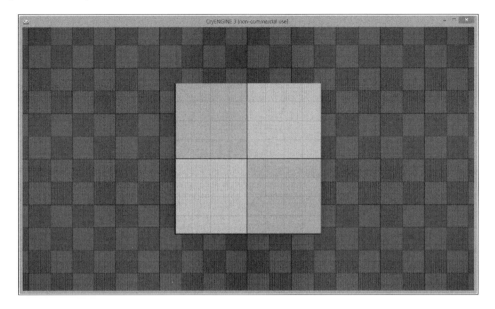

You should now have a basic understanding of how the player views function. To learn more, why not try and create your own camera, that is, an RPG-style isometric camera?

We can now move on to the next section, *Player input*.

Player inputs

Actors tend to be pretty boring when you can't control them. To aid in mapping events to inputs, we can make use of the following three systems:

System name	Description
IHardwareMouse	Used when there is a need for getting mouse events directly, such as x/y screen position and mousewheel delta.

System name	Description
IActionMapManager	Allows the registration of callbacks linked to key bindings. This is the preferred approach for keyboard and mouse button input due to it allowing each player to customize their preferred inputs via their action map profile.
	Action maps are commonly exposed via an in-game interface to simplify key mapping for the end user.
IInput	Used to listen to raw input events, for example, to detect when the Space bar was pressed or released.
	It is not recommended to use raw input except for rare edge cases such as chat and text input, instead action maps are preferable.

The hardware mouse

The hardware mouse implementation provides the `IHardwareMouseEventListener` struct to allow receiving mouse event callbacks. After deriving from and implementing its pure virtuals, use `IHardwareMouse::AddListener` to utilize it:

```
gEnv->pHardwareMouse->AddListener(this);
```

Listeners are most commonly called from constructors or initialization functions. Make sure you don't register listeners twice, and always remove them in your class destructor to prevent dangling pointers.

Action maps

Briefly mentioned in the table earlier, action maps allow binding keys to a named action. This is used to allow simple re-mapping of inputs from different game states. For example, if you have a game with two types of vehicles, you might not want the same keys to be used for both.

Action maps also allow changing the key an action is mapped to in real time. This allows the player to customize their preferred input methods.

Listening for action map events

The default action map profile is contained in `Game/Libs/Config/defaultProfile.xml`. When a game is released, the default profile is copied to the user's personal folder (typically in `My Games/Game_Title`) and can be modified by the user to remap keys, for example, to change which key triggers the **screenshot** action.

```xml
<profile version="0">
    <platforms>
        <PC keyboard="1" xboxpad="1" ps3pad="1" wiipad="0"/>
        <Xbox keyboard="1" xboxpad="1" ps3pad="0" wiipad="0"/>
        <PS3 keyboard="1" xboxpad="0" ps3pad="1" wiipad="0"/>
        <WiiU keyboard="1" xboxpad="0" ps3pad="0" wiipad="1" />
    </platforms>

    <actionmap name="debug" version="22">
    <!-- debug keys - move to debug when we can switch devmode-->
        <action name="flymode" onPress="1" noModifiers="1" keyboard="f3" />
        <action name="godmode" onPress="1" noModifiers="1" keyboard="f4" />
        <action name="toggleaidebugdraw" onPress="1" noModifiers="1" keyboard="f11" />
        <action name="togglepdrawhelpers" onPress="1" noModifiers="1" keyboard="f10" />
        <action name="ulammo" onPress="1" noModifiers="1" keyboard="np_2" />
        <action name="debug" onPress="1" keyboard="7" />
        <action name="thirdperson" onPress="1" noModifiers="1" keyboard="f1" xboxpad="xi_dpad_up" ps3pad="
        <action name="debug_next_actor" onPress="1" noModifiers="1" keyboard="backspace"/>
        <!-- debug keys - end -->
    </actionmap>

    <actionmap name="multiplayer" version="22">
    <!-- multiplayer specific keys -->
        <action name="radio_group_0" onPress="1" keyboard="f5" />
        <action name="radio_group_1" onPress="1" keyboard="f6" />
        <action name="radio_group_2" onPress="1" keyboard="f7" />
        <action name="radio_group_3" onPress="1" keyboard="f8" />
        <action name="scoreboard" onPress="1" keyboard="tab" xboxpad="xi_back" ps3pad="pad_select" wiipad=
    </actionmap>
```

To listen to action map events, we'll first have to either create a new action in the profile xml, or choose an existing one and modify it. For this example, we'll utilize the existing screenshot action.

IActionListener

The action map system provides the `IActionListener` struct to support providing callbacks for classes that require action map events.

Utilizing the listener is relatively easy:

1. Derive from the `IActorListener` struct.

2. Implement the `OnAction` event.

3. Register your listener:

```
gEnv->pGameFramework->GetIActionMapManager()-
    >AddExtraActionListener(this);
```

Listeners should only be registered once, which is why registration is preferred to take place in a constructor or initialization function.

Make sure to remove your listener when the class instance is destroyed.

Enabling action map sections

The action map system allows for creating several action map sections in the same profile, giving the game code the ability to toggle different action map sections in real time. This is very useful for games with multiple player states, such as walking and using vehicles. In that case, the vehicle and walking action maps would be contained in different sections that are then enabled/disabled while exiting or entering vehicles.

```
<actionmap name="walk" version="22">
  <action name="walkBack" onPress="1" keyboard="s" />
</actionmap>

<actionmap name="drive" version="22">
  <action name="break" onPress="1" keyboard="s" />
</actionmap>
```

To enable your custom action map, call `IActionMapManager::EnableActionMap`:

```
gEnv->pFramework->GetIActionMapManager()->EnableActionMap("walk",
  true);
```

This should be done at the precise moment the player should be able to receive these new actions. In the case of the previous example, enable the "walk" action when the player exits a vehicle.

Animated characters

`IAnimatedCharacter` is a game object extension which allows for locomotion and physics integration for objects. By using it, characters can request physical move requests, utilize animation graph functionality, and more.

As the extension is optional, it can be activated by any game object by simply acquiring it as explained in the *Chapter 3, Creating and Utilizing Custom Entities*

```
m_pAnimatedCharacter =
  static_cast<IAnimatedCharacter*>(GetGameObject()-
    >AcquireExtension("AnimatedCharacter"))
```

Once acquired, the animated character can be used right away.

 Animated character functionality such as movement requests require eEPE_OnPostStepImmediate physics events, which can be enabled via `IGameObject::EnablePhysicsEvent`.

Movement requests

When an animated character is physicalized as a living entity, it can request movement. This is essentially a wrapper for the pe_action_move physics request (see *Chapter 9, Physics Programming*, for more information) to allow simpler usage.

Character movement requests are very useful when dealing with advanced mechanics such as player movement.

 Note the difference between requesting movement, and simply setting the player position directly. By requesting velocity changes, we are able to have our entity react to collisions naturally.

Adding a movement request

To add movement requests, utilize `IAnimatedCharacter::AddMovement`, which requires a `SCharacterMoveRequest` object:

```
SCharacterMoveRequest request;

request.type = eCMT_Normal;
request.velocity = Vec3(1, 0, 0);
request.rotation = Quat(IDENTITY);

m_pAnimatedCharacter->AddMovement(request);
```

Seen in the previous code is a very basic example of a movement request, which will set the target on a course forward (world-space) indefinitely (if submitted continuously).

 Movement requests have to be added via the physics loop, see ENTITY_EVENT_PREPHYSICSUPDATE sent via `IGameObjectExtension::ProcessEvent`.

The Mannequin animation system

Introduced with CryENGINE 3.5 is the high-level Mannequin animation system. The system was designed with the goal of decoupling animation and game logic, effectively sitting as an additional layer between the CryAnimation module and the game code.

 Keep in mind that Mannequin can be applied to any entity, not just actors. However, Mannequin is integrated by default into the `IAnimatedCharacter` extension, making it easier for actors to utilize the new animation system.

Mannequin relies on a set of types that should be clearly understood before starting to use it:

Name	Description
Fragment	A fragment refers to a state, for example, "Landing". Each fragment can specify multiple animations on several layers, as well as a selection of effects.
	This allows for much smoother animations when dealing with, for example, first- and third-person views simultaneously. For that issue, each fragment would contain one full-body animation, one first-person, and then additional sounds, particles, and gameplay events.
Fragment ID	In order to avoid passing fragments directly, we can identify them by their Fragment ID.
Scope	Scopes allows the decoupling parts of characters in order to keep handle, for example, upper and lower body animations separately.
	While creating a new scope, each fragment will be able to add additional animations and effects to that scope to extend its behavior.
	For Crysis 3, the first- and third-person modes were declared as separate scopes in order to allow for the same fragments to handle both the states simultaneously.

Name	Description
Tag	Tags refer to a selection criteria, allowing subfragments to be selected based on the tags active.
	For example, if we have two fragments named "Idle" but one assigned to the "Injured" tag, we could dynamically switch between the two fragment variations based on if the player is injured or not.
Options	If we end up with multiple fragments that share the same identifier and tag, we have multiple options. The default behavior is to randomly select one of these options when the fragment is queried, effectively creating variation in the entity's animations.

The Mannequin Editor

The **Mannequin Editor** is used to tweak character animations and mannequin configuration in real-time via the Sandbox Editor.

Preview setup

The **Mannequin Editor** uses the preview files stored in `Animations/Mannequin/ Preview` in order to load a default model and animation database. When starting the **Mannequin Editor**, we need to load our preview setup by selecting **File | Load Preview Setup**.

Once loaded, we'll be given a visual representation of the preview setup, as shown in the following screenshot:

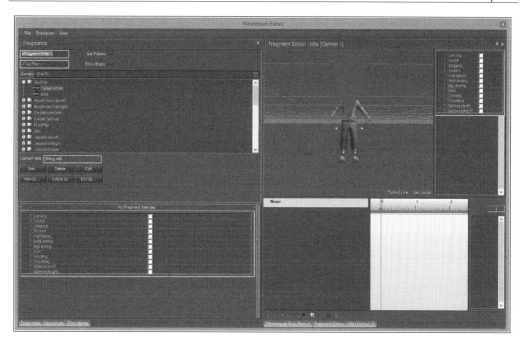

The contents of our preview file are as follows:

```
<MannequinPreview>
  <controllerDef
    filename="Animations/Mannequin/ADB/SNOWControllerDefinition.xml"/>
  <contexts>
    <contextData name="Char3P" enabled="1"
      database="Animations/Mannequin/ADB/Skiing.adb"
        context="Char3P" model="scripts/config/base.cdf"/>
  </contexts>
  <History StartTime="-4.3160208e+008" EndTime="-4.3160208e+008"/>
</MannequinPreview>
```

We'll be going through the details such as controller definitions, context data, and more, further into the chapter.

Creating contexts

As mentioned earlier in the chapter, contexts can be used to apply different animations and effects based on the character state.

We can create and modify contexts via the **Context Editor**, accessible by selecting **File | Context Editor** in the **Mannequin Editor**.

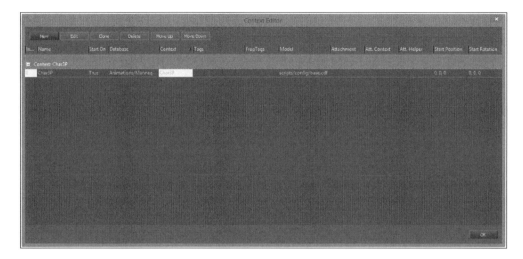

To create a new context, simply click on **New** in the upper-left corner, resulting in the **New Context** dialog being opened, as shown in the following screenshot:

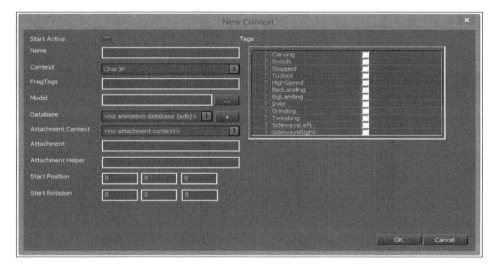

This allows us to tweak the context before creating it, including selecting which animation database and model to use.

When you're done, simply click on **OK** to see your context created.

Creating fragments

By default, we can see the fragments toolbox in the upper-left section of the **Mannequin Editor**. This tool is what we'll be using to create and edit fragments, in addition to adding or editing options.

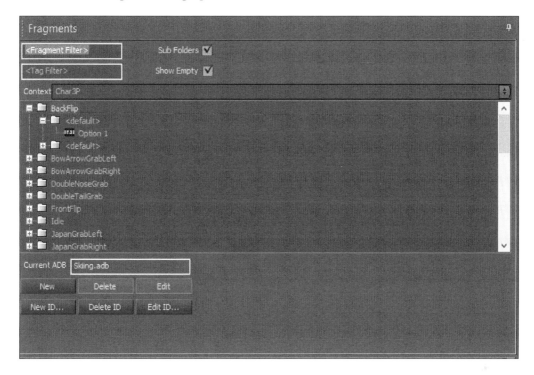

Seen in the previous screenshot is the fragments toolbox with the **BackFlip** fragment opened up, exposing two options.

To create a new fragment, click on the **New Id...** button, type in the desired name into the newly-opened message box, and then click on **OK**.

You should now see the **Mannequin FragmentID Editor** dialog as shown in the following screenshot:

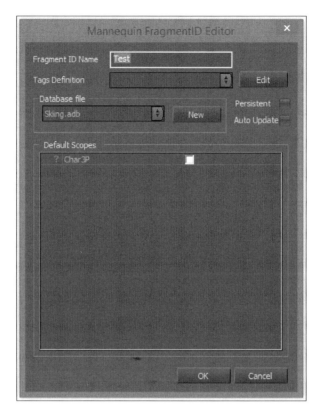

We'll now be able to select which scopes this fragment should run in. In our case, we simply need to check **Char3P** and click on **OK**.

You should now be able to see your fragment in the fragment toolbox:

Adding options

There are two methods to adding new options to your fragment:

- Open the Character Editor, select your animation and then drag it onto your Mannequin Fragment.
- Click the New button in the Fragment toolbox, and manually modify the option.

Creating and using tags

As mentioned earlier, the Mannequin system allows the creation of **Tags** that allow for selecting specific options for each Fragment based on if the tag is currently active or not.

To create a new Tag, open the Mannequin Editor and select **File -> Tag Definition Editor**:

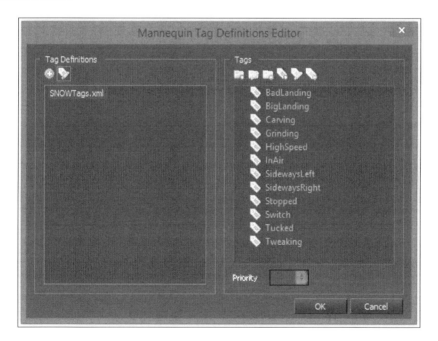

Once opened, you'll be presented with the **Mannequin Tag Definitions Editor**. The editor provides you with two sections: **Tag Definitions** and **Tags**.

The first thing we'll need to do is create a **Tag Definition**. This is a file that keeps track of a set of tags. To do so, press the plus (+) symbol in the **Tag Definitions** section and then specify the name of your definition.

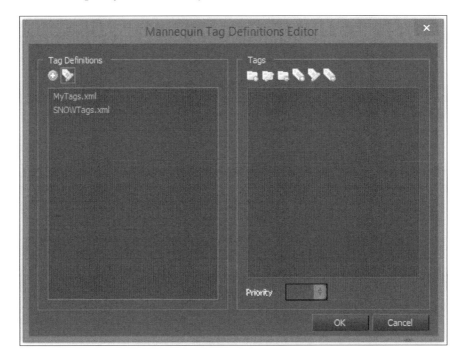

Great! You should now see your tag definition in the **Mannequin Tag Definitions Editor**. To create a new tag, select **MyTags.xml** and click on the tag creation icon (third from the right in the **Tags** section).

This presents you with a **Tag Creation** dialog in which you only need to specify the name of your tag. When you're done, click on **OK** and you should see the tag in the **Tags** section immediately (as shown in the following screenshot):

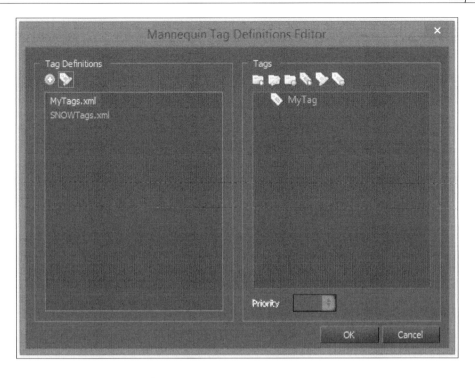

Appending tags to Options

Now that you have created your custom tag(s), we can select any fragment option in the Fragment Editor and then look a bit further down to find the Tag Toolbox:

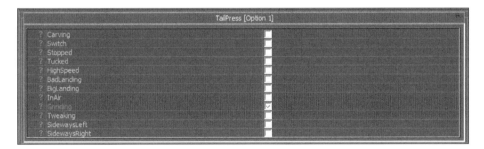

By simply selecting the checkbox next to each tag when a fragment option is selected, we tell the animation system that the option should be prioritized when the specified tag is active.

Saving

To save your **Mannequin Editor** changes, simply click on **File | Save Changes** and verify your changes in the **Mannequin File Manager** dialog that appears (as shown in the following screenshot):

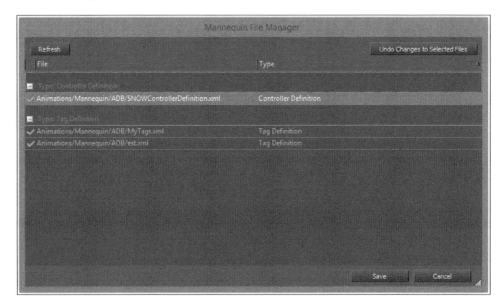

When you're ready to save, simply click on **Save** to have the system update the files.

Starting fragments

In C++, fragments are represented by the `IAction` interface that can be implemented or extended freely by each game if it is desired.

Queuing a fragment is done by calling the `IActionController::Queue` function, but before we do that we'll have to obtain our fragment's `FragmentId`.

Acquiring the fragment identifier

To acquire the fragment identifier, we'll have to get our current animation context in order to obtain the current controller definition, from which we can get the fragment ID:

```
SAnimationContext *pAnimContext = GetAnimatedCharacter()-
  >GetAnimationContext();
```

```
FragmentID fragmentId = pAnimContext-
  >controllerDef.m_fragmentIDs.Find(name);
CRY_ASSERT(fragmentId != FRAGMENT_ID_INVALID);
```

Note how we call `IAnimatedCharacter::GetAnimationContext`. As mentioned earlier in the chapter, the animated character extension implements Mannequin functionality for us.

Queuing the fragment

Now that we have the fragment identifier, we can simply create a new instance of the action we choose to use. In our case, we'll use the default Mannequin action exposed via the `TAction` template:

```
int priority = 0;
IActionPtr pAction = new TAction<SAnimationContext>(priority, id);
```

We now have our action, with priority 0. The animation system will compare the priority of queued actions in order to determine which should be used. For example, if two actions are queued simultaneously, with one having priority 0 and the other priority 1, the second action with priority 1 will be selected first.

Now to queue the action, simply call `IActionController::Queue`:

```
IActionController *pActionController = GetAnimatedCharacter()-
  >GetActionController();

pActionController->Queue(pAction);
```

Setting tags

To enable tags at runtime, we first have to obtain our tag's identifier as shown:

```
SAnimationContext *pAnimationContext = pActionController-
  >GetContext();

TagID tagId = pAnimationContext->state.GetDef().Find(name);
CRY_ASSERT(tagId != TAG_ID_INVALID);
```

Now we simply have to call `CTagState::Set`:

```
SAnimationContext *pAnimContext = pActionController->GetContext();

bool enable = true;
pAnimContext->state.Set(tagId, enable);
```

Done! Our tag is now activated, and will show as active in the animation system. If your action is set to update dynamically, it will select the appropriate option right away.

Forcing actions into requerying options

The default `IAction` implementation does not automatically select the relevant option when a tag is changed. To change this, we'll need to create a new class that derives from it and override its `Update` function with the following code:

```
IAction::EStatus CUpdatedAction::Update(float timePassedSeconds)
{
  TBase::Update(timePassedSeconds);

  const IScope &rootScope = GetRootScope();
  if(rootScope.IsDifferent(m_fragmentID, m_fragTags))
  {
    SetFragment(m_fragmentID, m_fragTags);
  }

  return m_eStatus;
}
```

What the previous code does is check when a better option is available, and select that instead.

Debugging Mannequin

To enable Mannequin debug, we'll need to append the `AC_DebugDraw` flag to the action controller:

```
pActionController->SetFlag(AC_DebugDraw, g_pGameCVars-
   >pl_debugMannequin != 0);
```

You are now presented with visual fragment and tag selection debug information. This is very useful when working with Mannequin.

Setting up Mannequin for a custom entity

As mentioned earlier in the chapter, the animated character game object extension integrates Mannequin by default. This is very handy when using actors, but in some cases it might be relevant to use the functionality Mannequin provides on custom entities.

To start, we'll need to store pointers to our action controllers and animation contexts in our entity extension as shown:

```
IActionController *m_pActionController;
SAnimationContext *m_pAnimationContext;
```

We'll then need to initialize Mannequin; this is commonly done in the game object extension's `PostInit` function.

Initializing Mannequin

The first thing to do is get the Mannequin interfaces:

```
// Mannequin Initialization
IMannequin &mannequinInterface = gEnv->pGame->GetIGameFramework()-
  >GetMannequinInterface();
IAnimationDatabaseManager &animationDBManager =
  mannequinInterface.GetAnimationDatabaseManager();
```

Loading the controller definition

Next, we have to load the controller definition we created for our entity:

```
const SControllerDef *pControllerDef =
  animationDBManager.LoadControllerDef("Animations/Mannequin/ADB/myC
    ontrollerDefinition.xml");
```

Great! Now that we have the controller definition, we can create our animation context with the following code:

```
m_pAnimationContext = new SAnimationContext(*pControllerDef);
```

We can now create our action controller:

```
m_pActionController =
  mannequinInterface.CreateActionController(pEntity,
    *m_pAnimationContext);
```

Setting the active context

Now that we have initialized our action controller, we'll need to set our default context.

To start, get the context identifier:

```
const TagID mainContextId = m_pAnimationContext-
  >controllerDef.m_scopeContexts.Find("Char3P");
```

```
CRY_ASSERT(mainContextId != TAG_ID_INVALID);
```

Then load the animation database we'll be using:

```
const IAnimationDatabase *pAnimationDatabase =
  animationDBManager.Load("Animations/Mannequin/ADB/myAnimDB.a
    db");
```

Once loaded, simply call `IActionController::SetScopeContext`:

```
m_pActionController->SetScopeContext(mainContextId, *pEntity,
  pCharacterInstance, pAnimationDatabase);
```

Once the context has been set, Mannequin is initialized and ready to process the queued fragments for your entity.

Remember that you can change scope context at any time using the `IActionController::SetScopeContext` function we used previously.

Summary

In this chapter, we learned how the actor system functions and created custom actors in C# and C++. By looking at the input and camera systems, we'll be able to handle basic player input and view setups.

You should also have a good understanding of the use cases of Mannequin, and how to set up custom entities to utilize them.

We now have all the core functionalities required for a game: flow nodes, entities, game rules, and actors. In the following chapters, we'll build upon existing knowledge and go into detail on how these systems can be used together.

If you want to continue working on actors before moving on, feel free to try and implement your own actor customized for a new scenario; for example, an isometric camera paired with basic RPG player elements.

In the next chapter, we'll be using the knowledge learned on actors to create **Artificial Intelligence (AI)**.

6
Artificial Intelligence

The CryENGINE AI system allows the creation of non-player controlled actors that roam the game world.

In this chapter we will:

- Learn how the AI system integrates with Lua scripts
- Discover what goal pipes are, and how to create them
- Use AI signals
- Register a custom AI `Actor` class
- Learn how to use behavior selection trees
- Create our own AI behavior

The Artificial Intelligence (AI) system

The CryENGINE AI system was designed to allow easy creation of custom AI actors flexible enough to handle a larger set of complex and different worlds.

Before we start looking into the native implementation of the AI system, we have to mention one very important fact: AI is not the same as an actor, and should never be confused as such.

In CryENGINE, AI still relies on an underlying actor implementation, commonly the exact same one as used by players. However, the implementation of the AI itself is done separately via the AI system, which in turn sends movemAent input, and so on to the actor.

Scripting

The main idea of CryENGINE's AI system is based on lots and lots of scripting. Instead of forcing programmers into modifying the complex CryAISystem module, it's possible to create new AI behaviors using Lua scripts contained in the `Scripts/AI` and `Scripts/Entities/AI` directories.

The AI system is currently largely hardcoded to usage of the `.lua` scripts, therefore we will not be able to use C# and C++ to any larger extent for AI development.

AI actors

As we mentioned previously, actors are separate from the AI itself. Essentially what this means is that we'll need to create an `IActor` implementation, and then specify which AI behavior the actor should use.

If your AI actors should behave roughly the same as your player, you should reuse the actor implementation.

As covered in the previous chapter, registering an actor can be done with the `REGISTER_FACTORY` macro. The only difference for AI actors is that the last parameters should be set to true instead of false:

```
REGISTER_FACTORY(pFramework, "MyAIActor", CMyAIActor, true);
```

Once registered, the AI system will search for a Lua script named after your entity in `Scripts/Entities/AI`. In the case of the previous snippet, the system would attempt to load `Scripts/Entities/AI/MyAIActor.lua`.

This script should contain a table of the same name, and functions the same as other Lua entities. For example, to add Editor properties, simply add variables inside a Properties subtable.

Goal pipes

Goal pipes define a collection of goal operations, allowing a set of goals to be triggered at runtime. For example, a goal pipe could entail the AI, increasing its movement speed while simultaneously beginning the search of player-controlled units.

Goal operations, such as LookAt, Locate, and Hide are created in `CryAISystem.dll` and cannot be modified without access to its source.

Creating custom pipes

Pipes are initially registered inside the `PipeManager:CreateGoalPipes` function in `Scripts/AI/GoalPipes/PipeManager.lua`, using the `AI.LoadGoalPipes` function:

```
AI.LoadGoalPipes("Scripts/AI/GoalPipes/MyGoalPipes.xml");
```

This snippet will load `Scripts/AI/GoalPipes/MyGoalPipes.xml`, which could contain the following goal pipe definition:

```
<GoalPipes>
  <GoalPipe name="myGoalPipes_findPlayer">
    <Locate name="player" />
    <Speed id="Run"/>
    <Script code="entity.Behavior:AnalyzeSituation(entity);"
  </GoalPipe>
</GoalPipes>
```

When this pipe is selected, the assigned AI will start locating the player, switch to the `Run` movement speed state, and call the `AnalyzeSituation` function contained in the currently selected behavior script.

Goal pipes can be very effective for pushing a set of goals easily, as an example based on the previous script, we could simply select the `myGoalPipes_findPlayer` pipe in order to have the AI run looking for the player.

Selecting pipes

Goal pipes are typically triggered using the entity function `SelectPipe` in Lua:

```
myEntity:SelectPipe(0, "myGoalPipe");
```

Or can otherwise be triggered via C++, using the `IPipeUser::SelectPipe` function.

Signals

In order to provide AI entities with an intuitive way of communicating with each other, we can use the signal system. Signals are events that can be sent to a specific AI unit from either another AI entity, or from another place in C++ or Lua code.

Signals can be sent using the `AI.Signal` function in Lua, or `IAISystem::SendSignal` in C++.

AI behaviors

Behaviors need to be assigned to each actor, and they define the decision making capabilities of the unit. By selecting behaviors at runtime using **behavior selection trees**, actors can give the impression of dynamically adjusting to their surroundings.

Behavior selection trees are created using XML files placed in `Scripts/AI/SelectionTrees`. Each tree manages a set of **behavior leaves**, each leaf representing a type of AI behavior that can be enabled based on conditions.

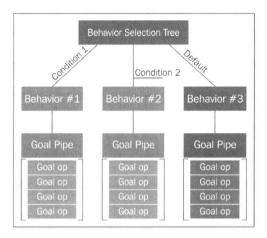

Sample

For example, see a very basic form of a selection tree XML definition as shown:

```
<SelectionTrees>
  <SelectionTree name="SelectionTreeSample"
    type="BehaviorSelectionTree">
    <Variables>
      <Variable name="IsEnemyClose"/>
    </Variables>
    <SignalVariables>
      <Signal name="OnEnemySeen" variable="IsEnemyClose"
        value="true"/>
      <Signal name="OnNoTarget" variable="IsEnemyClose"
        value="false"/>
      <Signal name="OnLostSightOfTarget" variable="IsEnemyClose"
        value="false"/>
    </SignalVariables>
    <LeafTranslations />
    <Priority name="Root">
```

```
      <Leaf name="BehaviorSampleCombat" condition="IsEnemyClose"/>
      <Leaf name="BehaviorSampleIdle"/>
    </Priority>
  </SelectionTree>
</SelectionTrees>
```

To allow for a better understanding of the sample, we'll break it down a bit:

```
<SelectionTree name="SelectionTreeSample"
  type="BehaviorSelectionTree">
```

This first snippet simply defines the name of the selection tree, and will be parsed by the AI system during AI initialization. If you want to rename your tree, simply change the name attribute:

```
<Variables>
  <Variable name="IsEnemyClose"/>
</Variables>
```

Each selection tree can define a set of variables that can be set either based on signals (see the next snippet), or inside each behavior script.

Variables are simply Boolean conditions that can be queried in order to determine which leaf or behavior to select next:

```
<SignalVariables>
  <Signal name="OnEnemySeen" variable="IsEnemyClose"
    value="true"/>
  <Signal name="OnNoTarget" variable="IsEnemyClose"
    value="false"/>
  <Signal name="OnLostSightOfTarget" variable="IsEnemyClose"
    value="false"/>
</SignalVariables>
```

Each behavior tree can also listen to signals such as OnEnemySeen, in order to set the value of variables easily. For example, in the snippet that we just saw, the IsEnemyClose variable will always be set to true when the enemy has been spotted, and then set to false when the target is lost.

We can then use the variable when querying for new leaves (see the following code snippet), allowing the AI to switch to different behavior scripts based on simple signal events:

```
<Priority name="Root">
  <Leaf name="BehaviorSampleCombat" condition="IsEnemyClose"/>
  <Leaf name="BehaviorSampleIdle"/>
</Priority>
```

By specifying leaves inside the `Priority` elements, we can enable behaviors (leaves) at runtime based on simple conditions.

As an example, the previous snippet will enable the `BehaviorSampleCombat` behavior script when an enemy is close, otherwise it will fall back to the `BehaviorSampleIdle` behavior.

> The behavior selection tree system will query leaves in order, and fall back to the last remaining leaf. In this case, it will query `BehaviorSampleCombat` first, and then fall back to `BehaviorSampleIdle` if the `IsEnemyClose` variable is set to false.

IAIObject

Entities that have been registered with the AI system can call `IEntity::GetAI` to obtain their `IAIObject` pointer.

By accessing the pointer to an entity's AI object, we can manipulate the AI at runtime, for example, to set custom signals that we later intercept in our AI behavior scripts:

```
if(IAIObject *pAI = pEntity->GetAI())
{
  gEnv->pAISystem->SendSignal(SIGNALFILTER_SENDER, 0,
    "OnMySignal", pAI);
}
```

Creating custom AI

The process of creating custom AI is relatively straightforward, especially if you're comfortable with the actor system introduced in the previous chapter.

There are two parts of each actor; its `IActor` implementation and the AI entity definition.

Registering an AI actor implementation

AI actors typically use the same IActor implementation as the player, or at least a shared derivation.

In C#

Registering an AI actor in C# is very similar to how we did it in *Chapter 5, Creating Custom Actors*. Essentially, all we have to do is derive from CryEngine.AIActor instead of CryEngine.Actor.

The AIActor class derives directly from Actor, and therefore does not sacrifice any of its callbacks and members. However, it has to be explicitly implemented in order to make CryENGINE treat this actor as if it is controlled by AI.

```
public class MyCSharpAIActor
: CryEngine.AIActor
{
}
```

You should now be able to place your entity from the **AI** category in the **Entity** browser, within Sandbox:

In C++

As with the C# actor that we just saw, registering an actor with the AI system is not much work. Simply derive from the actor implementation we created in the previous chapter:

```
class CMyAIActor
  : public CMyCppActor
{
};
```

Then open your GameDLL's `GameFactory.cpp` file and use the same setup for registering the actor, except the last parameter should be true to tell CryENGINE that this actor type will be controlled by AI:

```
REGISTER_FACTORY(pFramework, "MyAIActor", CMyAIActor, true);
```

Your actor should now be present in the **AI** entity category in the **Entity** browser, following a recompilation.

Creating the AI entity definition

When our AI actor is spawned, the AI system will search for an AI entity definition. The definitions exist to set default properties of an actor, for example, its Editor properties.

The first thing we need to do is open `Scripts/Entities/AI` and create a new `.lua` file with the same name as our `Actor` class. In our case, this will be `MyAIActor.lua` for the C++ implementation that we just created, and `MyCSharpAIActor.lua` for the C# actor.

The script is kept at a bare minimum of code, as we only need to load the base AI. The base AI is loaded using the `Script.ReloadScript` function.

By default, CryENGINE uses `Scripts/Entities/AI/Shared/BasicAI.lua` as the base AI definition. We will use a custom implementation, `Scripts/Entities/AI/AISample_x.lua` in order to cut down on unnecessary code that is irrelevant to this chapter:

```
Script.ReloadScript( "SCRIPTS/Entities/AI/AISample_x.lua");
----------------------------------------------------------------

MyCSharpAIActor = CreateAI(AISample_x);
```

That's it! Your AI is now properly registered, and should now be placeable via the Editor.

 For more information on the base AI definition, see the *AI base definition breakdown* section later on in this chapter.

AI behaviors and characters

As we spawn our custom AI actor, four entity properties should appear by default. These determine which systems the AI should use for decision making:

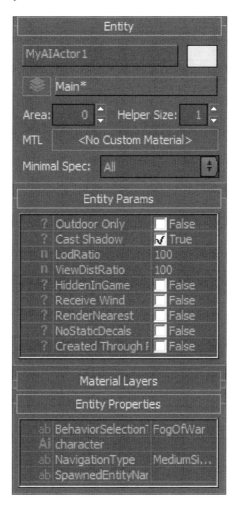

Understanding and using behavior selection trees

The behavior selection tree is the most important entity property for our AI actor, as it determines which behavior selection tree to use for the actor. If our project contains multiple behavior selection trees, we can easily spawn multiple AI actors that behave very differently due to the separate selection trees. The selection tree system exists in order to provide a way to query and select behavior scripts at runtime.

To see which trees are currently available, or to create your own, navigate to `Scripts/AI/SelectionTrees`. For our sample, we'll be using the `FogOfWar` selection tree present in `Scripts/AI/SelectionTrees/FogOfWar.xml`:

```xml
<SelectionTree name="FogOfWar" type="BehaviorSelectionTree">
  <Variables>
    <Variable name="IsFar"/>
    <Variable name="IsClose"/>
    <Variable name="AwareOfPlayer"/>
  </Variables>
  <SignalVariables>
    <Signal name="OnEnemySeen" variable="AwareOfPlayer"
      value="true"/>
    <Signal name="OnNoTarget" variable="AwareOfPlayer"
      value="false"/>
    <Signal name="OnLostSightOfTarget" variable="AwareOfPlayer"
      value="false"/>
  </SignalVariables>
  <LeafTranslations />
  <Priority name="Root">
    <Leaf name="FogOfWarSeekST" condition="IsFar"/>
    <Leaf name="FogOfWarEscapeST" condition="IsClose"/>
    <Leaf name="FogOfWarAttackST" condition="AwareOfPlayer"/>
    <Leaf name="FogOfWarIdleST"/>
  </Priority>
</SelectionTree>
```

Variables

Each selection tree exposes a set of variables that can be set at runtime. The variables will be queried by leaves in order to determine which behavior to activate.

Signal variables

Signal variables provide a simple way to set variables when signals are received.

For example, in the previous tree, we can see that `AwareOfPlayer` is dynamically set when the `OnEnemySeen` signal is received. The variables are then set to false when the AI loses track of the player.

Leaves / behavior queries

The leaves determine which behavior to play, based on a variable condition.

In the previous tree, we can see that the `FogOfWarIdleST` behavior is activated by default when all other conditions are set to false. However, say that the `IsFar` variable is set to true, the system will automatically switch to the `FogOfWarSeekST` behavior.

 Behaviors are loaded from the `Scripts/AI/Behaviors/Personalities/` directory, in our case, it'll find reference behaviors inside `Scripts/AI/Behaviors/Personalities/FogOfWarST/`.

Character

The `Character` property is used to set the AI character for our actor.

 In our sample, the `Character` property will default to an empty string, as the system is considered deprecated since the introduction of behavior selection trees (Have a look at the *Understanding and using behavior selection trees* section).

AI characters are contained in `Scripts/AI/Characters/Personalities` as the `.lua` scripts. For example, we could open and modify `Scripts/AI/Characters/Personalities/FogOfWar.lua` in order to modify our default personality.

You can also create new personalities simply by adding a new file in the `Personalities` directory, using `FogOfWar` as a baseline.

The `Character` property defines all applicable behaviors, in our case `FogOfWarAttack`, `FogOfWarSeek`, `FogOfWarEscape`, and `FogOfWarIdle`. The actor will be able to switch between these behaviors at runtime, based on internal and external conditions.

NavigationType

The `NavigationType` property determines which type of AI navigation to use. This allows the system to dynamically determine which paths are viable for the type of AI.

This defaults to MediumSizedCharacter in our sample, and can be set to any navigation definition contained in `Scripts/AI/Navigation.xml`.

Creating custom behaviors

We're almost done! The only step that remains is understanding how to create and modify AI behaviors, activated using the behavior selection tree we described previously.

To start, open `Scripts/AI/Behaviors/Personalities/FogOfWarST/ FogOfWarIdleST.lua` with the text editor of your choice. Due to the behavior tree setup described earlier, this is the behavior that will be activated when all other variables are set to false.

Behaviors are created by calling the `CreateAIBehavior` function, with the first parameter set to the name of the new behavior, and the second containing the behavior itself in a table.

Therefore, the bare minimum for a behavior would be:

```
local Behavior = CreateAIBehavior("MyBehavior",
{
  Alertness = 0,

  Constructor = function (self, entity)
  end,

  Destructor = function(self, entity)
  end,
})
```

This code snippet would set `Alertness` of the AI to 0 at all times, and does absolutely nothing when the behavior starts (`Constructor`) and ends (`Destructor`).

By looking at the `FogOfWarIdleST` behavior definition, we can see what it does:

```
Constructor = function (self, entity)
  Log("Idling...");
  AI.SetBehaviorVariable(entity.id, "AwareOfPlayer", false);
  entity:SelectPipe(0,"fow_idle_st");
end,
```

When the behavior is activated, we should see `Idling...` in the console, assuming that the log verbosity is set high enough (set using `log_verbosity` CVar).

After logging, the behavior will reset the `AwareOfPlayer` variable to false via the `AI.SetBehaviorVariable` function. We can use the function at any time to change the value of variables, effectively telling the behavior selection tree that another behavior should be queried.

After setting the variable to false, the constructor selects the `fow_idle_st` goal pipe.

Listening to signals

To listen to signals in behaviors, simply create a new function:

```
OnMySignal = function(self, entity, sender)

{

}
```

This will then be called when the `OnMySignal` signal is sent, along with the associated entity and behavior table.

AI base definition breakdown

Previously in the chapter, we created our own AI definition that relied on the `Scripts/Entities/AI/AISample_x.lua` base definition. This section will describe what the base definition does, in order to allow for a better understanding of the definition setup.

To start, open the definition with the text editor of your choice, for example, Notepad++.

The AISample_x table

The first lines of code we'll see when opening `AISample_x.lua` are its table definition, which defines each characters' default properties.

 Each AI definition can override properties set in the base definition.

The Properties table

The Properties table works as it does with the standard Lua entities, to define properties that appear when the entity is selected in the Editor.

 The default properties in our base AI definition are read from `CryAISystem.dll`. Removal of these properties is not supported, and will result in AI initialization failure.

The AIMovementAbility table

The `AIMovementAbility` subtable defines the movement capabilities of our actor, for example, walk and run speed.

The CreateAI function

The `CreateAI` function merges the base AI table with that of the specified child. This means that any table present in the AI base definition will be present in any AI definition that derives from it.

The `CreateAI` function also makes the entity spawnable, and exposes it to the network by calling the AI's `Expose()` function.

The RegisterAI function

The `RegisterAI` function is called when the actor should be registered with the AI system. This is called automatically on entity spawn and on editor property change.

Summary

In this chapter, we have learned about the core idea and implementation of the AI system and have created a custom AI actor implementation.

Having created our own AI entity definition, and behavior selection trees, you should be aware of how AI actors are created in the CryENGINE.

You should now have a good understanding of how to use the AI system to your advantage, allowing you to create AI-controlled units that patrol your game world.

If you're not quite done with AI, why not try and use your newly gained knowledge to create something a bit more complex of your own choice?

In the next chapter, we'll be covering the process of creating custom user interfaces allowing the creation of main menus and **Heads-up Display** (**HUD**).

7
The User Interface

CryENGINE integrates Scaleform GFx, allowing the rendering of Adobe Flash-based user interfaces, HUDs, and animated textures. By tying UI elements together at runtime using the UI flowgraph solution, developers can intuitively create and expand user interfaces in no time.

In this chapter we will cover the following topics:

- Learning about the CryENGINE Scaleform implementation, and the benefits it brings.
- Creating our main menu.
- Implementing a UI game event system

Flash movie clips and UI graphs

In order to provide developers with a solution for creating user interfaces, CryENGINE integrates Adobe Scaleform GFx, a real-time Flash renderer for game engines. The system allows the creation of user interfaces in Adobe Flash, which can then be exported for immediate use in the engine.

 It is also possible to use Flash `.swf` files in materials, allowing the rendition of Flash movie clips on 3D objects present in the game world.

The effort involved in creating modular dynamic user interfaces is greatly simplified with the addition of the UI flowgraph, a system that allows the creation and maintenance of any Flash UI element using the flowgraph system.

The UI flowgraph system is based on the concept of two types: **elements** and **actions**. Each element represents a Flash file (`.swf` or `.gfx`), while each action is one flowgraph representing a UI state.

Elements

UI elements are configured via XML files in `Game/Libs/UI/UIElements/`, and represent each Flash file. By modifying the UI element's configuration, we can change the events it receives and alignment mode, as well as expose the different functions and callbacks present in the exported SWF file.

XML Breakdown

The bare minimum for an element can be seen in the following code:

```xml
<UIElements name="Menus">
  <UIElement name="MyMainMenu" mouseevents="1" keyevents="1"
    cursor="1" controller_input="1">

    <GFx file="Menus_Startmenu.swf" layer="3">
      <Constraints>
        <Align mode="fullscreen" scale="1"/>
      </Constraints>
    </GFx>

    <functions>
    </functions>

    <events>
    </events>
    <Arrays>
    </Arrays>

    <MovieClips>
    </MovieClips>
  </UIElement>
</UIElements>
```

The previous XML code can be saved as `Game/Libs/UI/UIElements/ MyMainMenu.xml`, and will load the Flash file called `Menus_Startmenu.swf` in the `Game/Libs/UI/` folder.

Once created, we'll be able to select our new UI element via flowgraph nodes such as **UI:Display:Config** (used to reconfigure any element in order to, for example, enable mouse events for an element at runtime).

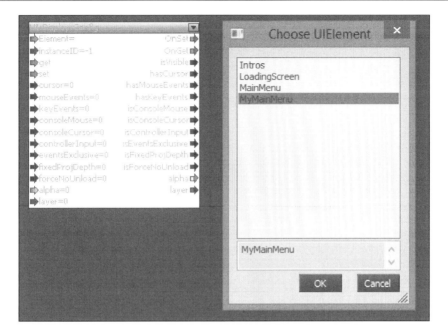

Now that we know it works, let's break it down a bit:

```
<UIElements name="Menus">
```

This first element defines the start of the file, and determines in which category our element should be placed.

```
<UIElement name="MyMainMenu" mouseevents="1" keyevents="1"
  cursor="1" controller_input="1">
```

The UIElement XML element is used to decide the initial configuration, including the default name, and determining which events should be received by default.

As seen previously, each element can be configured via a set of attributes, allowing the developer to define what type of events to listen to:

Attribute name	Description
name	Defines the name of the element (String).
mouseevents	Determines whether mouse events are sent to the Flash file (0/1).
cursor	Determines whether to display a cursor while the element is visible (0/1).
keyevents	Determines whether to send key events to the Flash file (0/1).

Attribute name	Description
console_mouse	Determines whether the thumbstick should function as a cursor on console hardware (0/1).
console_cursor	Determines whether to display a cursor while the element is visible while running on console hardware (0/1).
layer	Defines the order in which the elements are displayed, in case multiple elements are present.
alpha	Sets the background alpha of the element (0-1).
	Allows transparency in-game, for example, to feature an in-game level behind your main menu.

 Note that the previously mentioned properties can be tweaked in real time by using the **UI:Display:Config** node.

```
<GFx file="Menus_Startmenu.swf" layer="3">
```

The GFx element determines which Flash file should be loaded for the element. It is possible to load multiple GFx files and put them into different layers.

This allows for selecting which element layer to use at runtime, for example, via the layer input on the **UI:Display:Config** node shown in the previous screenshot.

```
<Constraints>
  <Align mode="fullscreen" scale="1"/>
</Constraints>
```

Constraints allow configuring how the GFx element is displayed on screen, giving the developer the ability to tweak how the element performs under different display resolutions.

There are currently three modes as follows:

Mode name	Description	Additional attributes
fixed	In the fixed mode, the developer can use four attributes to set the pixel distance from top and left corners, as well as set the desired resolution.	top, left, width, and height
dynamic	In dynamic mode, the element is aligned on anchors, allowing horizontal and vertical alignment.	halign, valign, scale, and max
	halign can be set to left, center, or right, while valign can be set to top, center, or bottom.	
	If scale is set to 1, the element will be scaled to the screen resolution while maintaining aspect ratio.	
	If max is set to 1, the element will be maximized to make sure that 100 percent of the screen is covered.	
fullscreen	When active in this mode, the element viewport will be exactly the same as the render viewport.	scale
	If scale is set to 1, the element will be stretched to the screen resolution.	

Actions

UI actions are the core of the UI flowgraph implementation. Each action is represented by a flowgraph, and defines a UI state. For example, each screen in a main menu would be handled using a separate action.

All available UI actions can be seen in the **Flow Graphs** toolbox, inside the Flowgraph Editor.

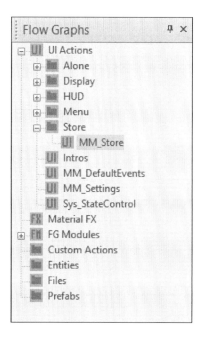

To create a new UI action, navigate to **File | New UI action**, and specify the name of your new action in the newly opened **Save As** dialog box:

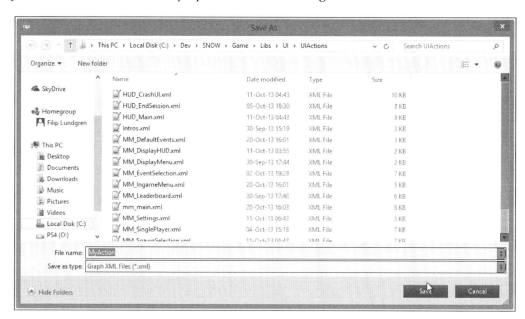

Actions are started by using the **UI:Action:Control** node and specifying the name of the pending action in the **UIAction** input port, and then activating the **Start** input.

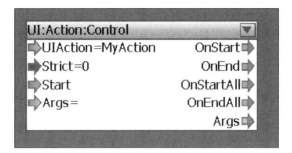

Once started, the UI graph with the specified name will be activated, assuming it contains a **UI:Action:Start** node as shown:

The graph can then initialize the requested UI by listening to the **StartAction** output port. Once the action is done, it should call **UI:Action:End** as shown:

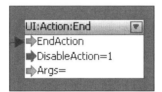

And that's it. UI graphs are saved as flowgraph XML files in `Game/Libs/UI/UIActions/`. The initial UI action is called **Sys_StateControl** and will always be active. The state controller graph should be responsible for loading and enabling menus based on system events such as level load.

The system state control action (`Sys_StateControl.xml`) is always active, and is used to start the initial actions, for example, to display the main menu when the engine is started.

Creating a main menu

Now that we have a basic understanding of the UI flowgraph implementation, let's get started with creating our very own main menu.

Creating menu elements

The first thing we need to do is create our UI element definition in order to provide the engine with a means for loading our exported SWF file.

To do so, create a new XML document in `Game/Libs/UI/UIElements/` named `MainMenuSample.xml`. The bare minimum code required for our menu can be seen in the following code:

```
<UIElements name="Menus">
  <UIElement name="MainMenuSample" mouseevents="1" keyevents="1"
    cursor="1" controller_input="1">
    <GFx file="MainMenuSample.swf" layer="3">
      <Constraints>
        <Align mode="dynamic" halign="left" valign="top" scale="1"
          max="1"/>
      </Constraints>
    </GFx>
  </UIElement>
</UIElements>
```

With the previous code present, the engine will know where to load our SWF file, and how to align it on the screen.

> SWF files can be re-exported by using `GFxExport.exe` (usually present in the `<root>/Tools/` directory) to be more efficient for an in-engine use. This is usually done before releasing the game.

Exposing ActionScript assets

Moving on, we'll need to expose the functions and events we defined in our Flash source file in order to allow the engine to invoke and receive these.

When exposing functions and events, we create simplistic flowgraph nodes that can be used by any flowgraph.

Once created, function nodes can be accessed by navigating to **UI | Functions** as shown in the following screenshot:

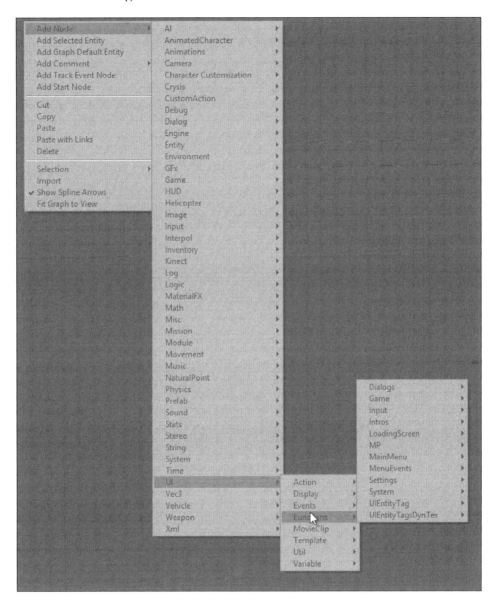

Events can be found by navigating to **UI** | **Events**.

 It is also possible to create UI actions and elements in C++, effectively giving the user interface the ability to send and get events from native code. We'll be going through this in the *Creating UI Game Event System* section later in this chapter.

Functions

To expose a method, we need to add a new `<functions>` section into the `UIElement` definition as shown in the following code:

```
<functions>
  <function name="SetupScreen" funcname="setupScreen" desc="Sets
    up screen, clearing previous movieclips and configuring
      settings">
    <param name="buttonX" desc="Initial x pos of buttons"
      type="int" />
    <param name="buttonY" desc="Initial y pos of buttons"
      type="int" />
    <param name="buttonDividerSize" desc="Size of the space
      between buttons" type="int" />
  </function>

  <function name="AddBigButton" funcname="addBigButton" desc="Adds
    a primary button to the screen">
    <param name="id" desc="Button Id, sent with the onBigButton
      event" type="string" />
    <param name="title" desc="Button text" type="string" />
  </function>
</functions>
```

Using the previous code, the engine will create two nodes that we can utilize to invoke the `setupScreen` and `addBigButton` ActionScript methods from our UI Graphs.

 Functions are always placed in the same flowgraph category: **UI:Functions:ElementName:FunctionName**

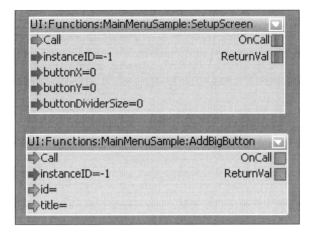

When the **Call** port on either of the nodes displayed in the previous screenshot is triggered, the ActionScript method will be invoked with the specified parameters.

 The **instanceID** input port determines which element instance to invoke the function on. If the value is set to -1 (default), it will be invoked on all instances, otherwise if set to -2, it will be called on all initialized instances.

Events

Setting up events is done in a similar way to functions, by using the `<events>` tag as shown:

```
<events>
  <event name="OnBigButton" fscommand="onBigButton"
    desc="Triggered when a big button is pressed">
    <param name="id" desc="Id of the button" type="string" />
  </event>
</events>
```

The previous code will result in the engine making the **OnBigButton** node available, triggered when the Flash file invokes the `onBigButton` fscommand, along with the associated button ID.

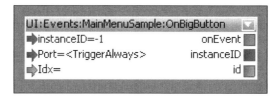

Invoking a `fscommand` from Flash is relatively easy. The following code will trigger the `onBigButton` event, along with the associated button ID string.

```
fscommand("onBigButton", buttonId);
```

 Similar to functions, events are always placed in **UI:E vents:ElementName:EventName**.

Variables

It's also possible to define access to variables present in the Flash source file via the element definition. This allows for getting and setting the value of your variable by using the **UI:Variable:Var** node.

To start, define your array inside the element definition's `<variables>` block:

```
<variables>
  <variable name="MyTextField"
    varname="_root.m_myTextField.text"/>
</variables>
```

After restarting the editor, place a new **UI:Variable:Var** node and browse for your new variable as shown in the following screenshot:

Then we can simply set or get the value of our variable at any time by using flowgraph:

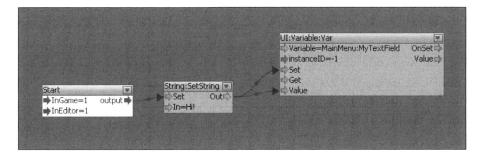

Arrays

In the previous section, we set the value of a Flash variable at runtime. This is also possible for arrays, by using the **UI:Variable:Array** node.

To start, expose the array inside your element's `<arrays>` block as shown:

```
<arrays>
  <array name="MyArray" varname="_root.m_myArray"/>
</arrays>
```

Then simply restart your array and repeat the previous process, but with the **UI:Variable:Array** node. To create a new array via your UI graph, use the **UI:Util:ToArray** node:

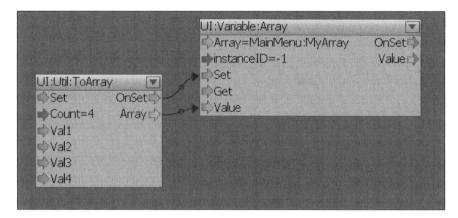

Exposing MovieClip instances to flowgraph

In the same way that variables can be exposed, it's also possible to give direct access to MovieClips via the UI graphs. This allows the possibility to go to specific frames, change properties, and more.

All nodes that allow MovieClip interaction can be found by navigating to **UI | MovieClip** within the Flowgraph Editor: as shown in the following screenshot:

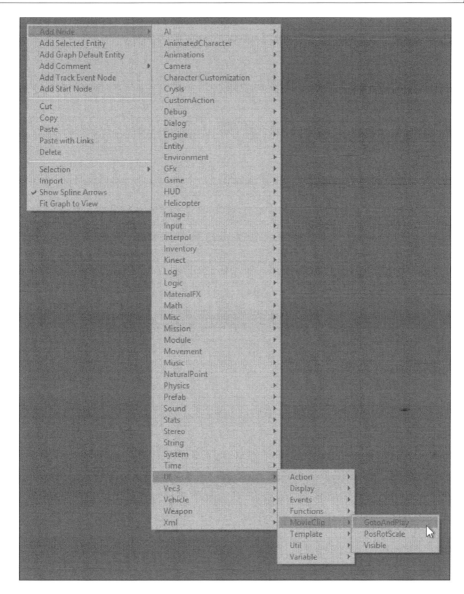

To start, add or edit the `<movieclips>` block in your element definition as shown:

```
<movieclips>
  <movieclip name="MyMovieClip"
    instancename="_root.m_myMovieclip"/>
</movieclips>
```

This will give flowgraph access to the **m_myMovieClip** movieclip present in your Flash file.

Once the editor has been restarted, we can, for example, use the **UI:MovieClip:GotoAndPlay** node to skip directly to a different frame in the specified clip as shown in the following screenshot:

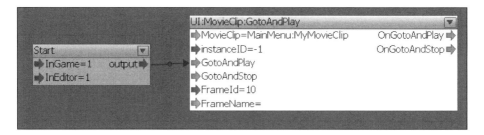

Creating the UI actions

Now that we've configured the main menu element, it's time to create the UI actions that will result in the menu appearing in the Launcher application.

Creating the state control graph

Start by opening Sandbox and the Flowgraph Editor. Once it is open, create a new UI action by navigating to **File | New UI Action**. Call the action **Sys_StateControl**. This will be the primary UI action in which we trigger the initial menu and handle crucial system events.

Once the action has been created, we'll be using the following three system events:

- OnSystemStarted
- OnLoadingError
- OnUnloadComplete

Together, these events signify when our main menu should appear. We'll be tying them together into a **UI:Action:Control** node, which in turn activates the MainMenu UIAction we'll create later.

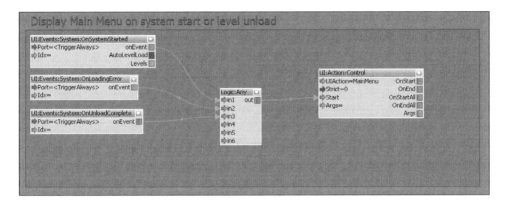

Creating the MainMenu action

When you're done, create another UI action and name it **MainMenu**. Once this is open, place a **UI:Action:Start** node. It's **StartAction** output port will be automatically activated when the **UI:Action:Control** node we created previously is executed.

We can now hook the **Start** node to a **UI:Display:Display** and **UI:Display:Config** node in order to initialize the main menu, making sure that the user can see it.

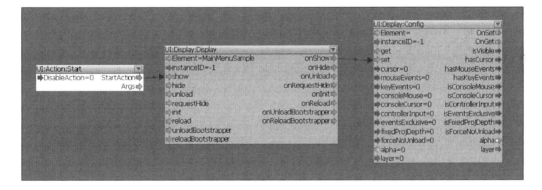

Our flash file will now be displayed when the game starts, but currently lacks any additional configuration from flowgraph.

Adding buttons

Now that our main menu file is initialized, we'll need to add a bit of ActionScript code to the Flash file in order to allow dynamic spawning and handling of buttons from our UI graph.

This section assumes that you have a MovieClip that you can instantiate at runtime. In our sample, we'll be using a custom button called **BigButton**.

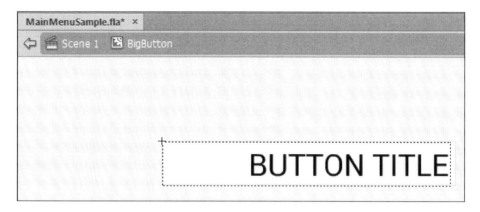

 The Flash source file (`.fla`) for our main menu is present in the `Game/Libs/UI/` folder of our sample installation, downloadable from `https://github.com/inkdev/CryENGINE-Game-Programming-Sample/`.

This section also assumes that you have two ActionScript functions: `SetupScreen` and `AddBigButton`.

`SetupScreen` should configure the default settings for the scene, and remove all previously spawned objects. In our case, we want buttons spawned using `AddBigButton` to be removed whenever we call `SetupScreen`.

`AddBigButton` should simply be a function that spawns a pre-created button instance as shown:

```
var button = _root.attachMovie("BigButton", "BigButton" +
  m_buttons.length, _root.getNextHighestDepth());
```

When the button is clicked on, it should invoke an event that we catch in flowgraph:

```
fscommand("onBigButton", button._id);
```

For information on creating functions and events, see the *Exposing ActionScript assets* section discussed earlier.

When you're done, add the nodes to your MainMenu action, and call them after configuring the element:

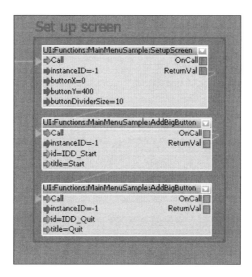

Our main menu should now appear when starting the Launcher application, but there's no feedback for any user interaction with it.

To resolve this, we can utilize the OnBigButton node that we exposed earlier in the chapter. This node will send events when a button has been clicked on, along with a string identifier that we can use to figure out which node was clicked:

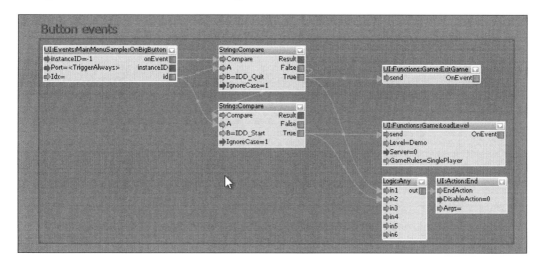

In the previous graph, we intercept the button events and use the **String:Compare** node to check what we need to do with the input. If the **IDD_Quit** button was clicked, we exit the game, and if the **IDD_Start** node was clicked, we load the **Demo** level.

End result

Assuming that you didn't create your own menu design, you should now see the following screenshot when starting the Launcher:

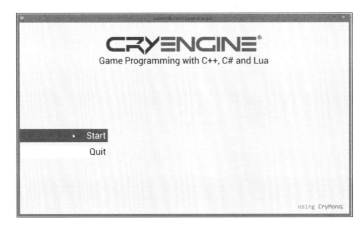

Now that you've learned how easy creating a simple menu is, why not go ahead and create a **Heads-Up Display (HUD)** that is shown when the player is spawned?

Engine ActionScript callbacks

There are a number of ActionScript callbacks that are automatically called by the engine. Simply by defining the functions in your Flash source file root, the engine will be able to invoke them.

- `cry_onSetup(isConsole:Boolean)`: This function is called when the SWF file is initially loaded by the engine.

- `cry_onShow()`: This function is called when the SWF file is shown.

- `cry_onHide()`: This function is called when the SWF file is hidden.

- `cry_onResize(_iWidth:Number, _iHeight:Number)`: This function is called when the in-game resolution is changed.

- `cry_onBack()`: This function is called when the user presses the back button.

- `cry_requestHide()`: This function is called when the element is hidden.

Creating UI game event systems

The UI system utilizes the `IUIGameEventSystem` interface to communicate with flowgraph, allowing for custom functions and events to be defined in the same manner in which the ActionScript assets are exposed.

This is used to allow user interfaces to access game and engine functionalities such as getting a list of playable levels. Each game event system specifies its category, which is then used in the Flowgraph Editor to define the category of functions and events registered.

For example, if we create an event system named MyUI using `IFlashUI::CreateEventSystem`, all functions will be found by navigating to **UI** | **Functions** | **MyUI**.

Implementing IUIGameEventSystem

Implementing `IUIGameEventSystem` doesn't require much work; there are only the following three pure virtuals that we need to assign:

- `GetTypeName`: This is not directly overridden; use the `UIEVENTSYSTEM` macro instead.
- `InitEventSystem`: This is called to initialize the event system.
- `UnloadEventSystem`: This is called to unload the event system.

Therefore, the bare minimum is as follows (the following file was saved as `MyUIGameEventSystem.h`):

```
class CMyUIGameEventSystem
  : public IUIGameEventSystem
{
public:
  CMyUIGameEventSystem() {}

  // IUIGameEventSystem
  UIEVENTSYSTEM("MyUIGameEvents");
  virtual void InitEventSystem() {}
  virtual void UnloadEventSystem() {}
  // ~IUIGameEventSystem
};
```

Now that we have the class definition resolved, we can move on to the code itself. Start by creating a new file called `MyUIGameEventSystem.cpp`.

Once this file is created, register the event system by using the REGISTER_UI_ EVENTSYSTEM macro. This is used to automatically create an instance of your class from within the CUIManager class.

Place the macro at the bottom of your CPP file, outside of the method scope as shown:

```
REGISTER_UI_EVENTSYSTEM(CMyUIGameEventSystem);
```

 Note that the REGISTER_UI_EVENTSYSTEM macro will only work in the CryGame project.

Our event system should now compile, and will be created along with the other event systems contained in CryGame.

Our event system doesn't do anything at the moment. Read the following sections to learn how to expose functions and events to the UI flowgraphs.

Receiving events

Event systems can expose functions that work in the same way that the nodes we registered via our Main Menu element do. By exposing functions, we can allow the graphs to interact with our game to, for example, request player health.

To start, we'll need to add two new members to our CMyUIGameEventSystem class:

```
SUIEventReceiverDispatcher<CMyUIGameEventSystem> m_eventReceiver;
IUIEventSystem *m_pUIFunctions;
```

The event dispatcher will be responsible for invoking functions as their nodes are triggered in flowgraph.

To start creating a function, add the following code to the class declaration:

```
void OnMyUIFunction(int intParameter)
{
  // Log indicating whether the call was successful
  CryLogAlways("OnMyUIFunction %i", intParameter);
}
```

To register our function, add the following code within your InitEventSystem function:

```
// Create and register the incoming event system
m_pUIFunctions = gEnv->pFlashUI->CreateEventSystem("MyUI",
  IUIEventSystem::eEST_UI_TO_SYSTEM);
```

```
m_eventReceiver.Init(m_pUIFunctions, this, "MyUIGameEvents");

// Register our function
{
  SUIEventDesc eventDesc("MyUIFunction", "description");

  eventDesc.AddParam<SUIParameterDesc::eUIPT_Int>("IntInput",
    "parameter description");

  m_eventReceiver.RegisterEvent(eventDesc,
    &CMyUIGameEventSystem::OnMyUIFunction);
}
```

You should now be able to see your node in the Flowgraph Editor after recompiling and restarting Sandbox:

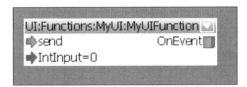

Dispatching events

Being able to expose events to the UI graph is very useful, allowing you to handle event-based UI logic to, for example, display a scoreboard when the user requests it.

To start off, lets add the following code to your class:

```
enum EUIEvent
{
    eUIE_MyUIEvent
};

SUIEventSenderDispatcher<EUIEvent> m_eventSender;
IUIEventSystem *m_pUIEvents;
```

The EUIEvent enum contains the various events we're going to register, and is used as a way for the event sender to know which event you're trying to send to the UI system.

Now we'll need to append a bit of code to the `InitEventSystem` function to expose our event as shown:

```
// Create and register the outgoing event system
m_pUIEvents = gEnv->pFlashUI->CreateEventSystem("MyUI",
IUIEventSystem::eEST_SYSTEM_TO_UI);

m_eventSender.Init(m_pUIEvents);

// Register our event
{
    SUIEventDesc eventDesc("OnMyUIEvent", "description");
    eventDesc.AddParam<SUIParameterDesc::eUIPT_String>("String",
"String output description");
    m_eventSender.RegisterEvent<eUIE_MyUIEvent>(eventDesc);
}
```

The **OnMyUIEvent** node should now appear in the Editor after a successful recompilation:

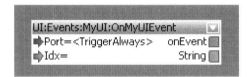

Dispatching the event

To dispatch your UI event, use `SUIEventSenderDispatcher::SendEvent`:

```
m_eventSender.SendEvent<eUIE_MyUIEvent>("MyStringParam");
```

Summary

In this chapter, we have learned how user interfaces are created in CryENGINE, and created our own main menu with that knowledge.

You know have the basic knowledge required to implement your own UI and UI event systems..

If you would prefer to work more with user interfaces before moving on to the next chapter, why not expand the Main Menu we created earlier? A good starting point could be to implement a level selection screen.

In the next chapter, we'll be covering the process of creating networked games to allow multiplayer functionality.

8
Multiplayer and Networking

Using the CryENGINE networking system, we can move on from single player games and create living worlds with large numbers of human players.

In this chapter, we will:

- Learn the basics of the network system
- Utilize Remote Method Invocations (RMIs)
- Serialize flowing data over the network using aspects

The networking system

The CryENGINE networking implementation is a flexible setup used to communicate with game servers and other clients.

All network messages are sent from an **independent networking thread** in order to avoid network updates being crippled by the game frame rate.

Network identifiers

Locally, each entity is represented by an entity identifier (`entityId`). However, for network contexts, it is not viable to transmit these over the network as they are not guaranteed to point to the same entity on the remote client or server.

To resolve this, each game object is assigned a net object identifier represented by the `SNetObjectID` struct, which contains a simple wrapper for the identifier and its salt.

When writing game code that serializes entities and entity IDs across the network, we don't have to deal with `SNetObjectID` structs directly as the process of converting `entityId` to `SNetObjectID` (and back to `entityId` on the remote machine) is automatic.

To make sure that your entity ID maps to the same entity on the remote machine, use the `eid` compression policy when serializing. Read more about policies and how to use them in the *Compression policies* section, later in this chapter.

Net channels

CryENGINE provides the `INetChannel` interface to represent an ongoing connection between two machines. For example, if client A and client B need to communicate with each other, a net channel is created on both machines to manage sent and received messages.

Each channel is referred to by using a channel identifier, which often proves useful to determine which client belongs to what machine. For example, to retrieve the player actor connected on a specific channel, we use `IActorSystem::GetActorByChannelId`.

Net nubs

All net channels are handled by the `INetNub` interface, which consists of one or more ports for packet-based communication.

Setting up a multiplayer game

To set up a multiplayer game, we'll need two computers running the same build of your game.

Starting the server

There are two methods to create a server that remote clients can connect to. These are explained as follows:

Dedicated server

The dedicated server exists for the purpose of having a client that does not render or play back audio, to allow full focus on supporting a server without a local client.

To start a dedicated server, perform the following steps:

1. Start `Bin32/DedicatedServer.exe`.
2. Type in `map` followed by the name of the level you want to load, and then press *Enter*.

Launcher

It is also possible to start a server via the Launcher, effectively allowing you to play with friends without having to launch a separate server application.

To start a server via the Launcher, follow these steps:

1. Start your Launcher application.
2. Open the console.

3. Type in map <level name> s.

 Appending s to the map command will tell the CryENGINE to load the level in a multiplayer context as the server. Leaving out s will still load the level, but in a single player state.

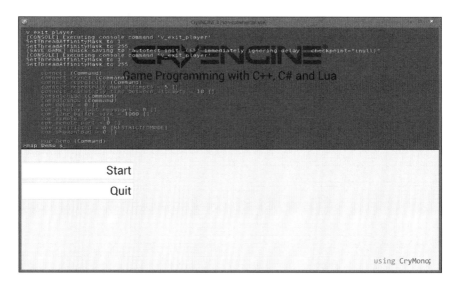

Connecting to a server via the console

To connect to a server using the console, use the connect command:

- connect <ip> <port>

 The default connection port is 64089.

It is also possible to set the IP address via the cl_serveraddr console variable, the port via cl_serverport, and then simply calling connect.

 Remember that you can have multiple Launchers running simultaneously, which can be very useful when debugging multiplayer games.

Debugging networked games

A very useful console variable to use when debugging networked games is `netlog 1`, which will result in the network system logging a lot more information about network issues and events in the console.

Networking using game object extensions

Game objects have two methods of communicating over the network: RMIs and network serialization via `Aspects`. Essentially, RMIs allow for event-based data transmission over the network, whereas an aspect continuously synchronizes data as it is invalidated.

Prior to being able to communicate over the network, each game object has to be bound to the network by using the `IGameObject::BindToNetwork` function. This can be called from your `Init` implementation by `IGameObjectExtension`.

Remote Method Invocation (RMI)

Remote Method Invocation (RMI) is used to invoke functions on a remote client or server. This is very useful for synchronizing a state over the network, for example, to let all clients know that the player named "Dude" just spawned, and should be moved to a specific location and orientation.

RMI structure

To declare an RMI, we can make use of the macros listed as shown:

- `DECLARE_SERVER_RMI_NOATTACH`
- `DECLARE_CLIENT_RMI_NOATTACH`
- `DECLARE_SERVER_RMI_PREATTACH`
- `DECLARE_CLIENT_RMI_PREATTACH`
- `DECLARE_SERVER_RMI_POSTATTACH`
- `DECLARE_CLIENT_RMI_POSTATTACH`

An example being:

```
DECLARE_CLIENT_RMI_NOATTACH(ClMoveEntity, SMoveEntityParams, eNRT_
ReliableUnordered);
```

> The last parameter specifies packet reliability, but is largely deprecated in the latest version of CryENGINE.
>
> Keep in mind which type of RMI you are exposing when it is created. For example, DECLARE_CLIENT is only used for functions that will be called on remote clients, whereas DECLARE_SERVER defines functions that will be called on the server, after being requested on a client.

Parameters

The RMI declaration macros require three parameters to be supplied:

- **Function name**: This is the first parameter that determines the name of the method, and is what will be used for the function declaration and when invoking the RMI itself.

- **RMI parameters**: The RMI has to specify a struct containing all members that will be serialized along with the method. The struct must contain a function named SerializeWith which accepts one TSerialize parameter.

- **Packet delivery reliability enum**: This is the last parameter that defines reliability of the packet delivery.

There are three types of differences between the macros that we just saw:

Attach type

The attachment type defines when the RMI is attached during the network serialization:

- NOATTACH: This is used when the RMI doesn't rely on game object data, and can therefore be attached either prior to or after game object data serialization.

- PREATTACH: In this type, the RMI will be attached before the game object data is serialized. It is used when the RMI needs to prepare for incoming data.

- POSTATTACH: In this type, the RMI is attached after the game object's data is serialized. It is used when the newly-received data is relevant to the RMI.

Server/client separation

As you may have noticed from looking at the RMI declaration macros, an RMI cannot target both clients and servers at the same time.

Because of this, we'll either have to decide which target should be able to run our function, or create one macro for each target.

This is a very useful feature when dealing with server-authoritative game contexts, due to the continuous distinction between functions that can be remotely triggered on the server and clients.

Function definition

To define the RMI function, we can use the `IMPLEMENT_RMI` macro:

```
IMPLEMENT_RMI(CGameRules, ClMoveEntity)
{

}
```

The macro defines a function called when the RMI is invoked, with two parameters:

- `params`: This contains the deserialized data sent from the remote machine.
- `pNetChannel`: This is an `INetChannel` instance which describes the connection established between the source and target machines.

RMI example

To demonstrate how to create a basic RMI, we're going to create an RMI to allow clients to request that an entity is repositioned. This will result in the server sending a `ClMoveEntity` RMI to all clients, notifying them of the new entity.

First, we'll need to open our header file. This is where we'll define the RMI and our parameters. Start by creating a new struct called `SMoveEntityParams`.

We'll then add three parameters:

- **EntityID entityId**: This is the identifier of the entity that we want to move
- **Vec3 position**: This determines which position the entity should be moved to
- **Quat orientation**: This is used to set the rotation of the entity on spawn

After adding the parameters, we need to define the `SerializeWith` function inside our `SMoveEntityParams` struct. This will be called when sending data to the network, and again to receive the data.

```
void SerializeWith(TSerialize ser)
{
  ser.Value("entityId", entityId, 'eid');
  ser.Value("position", position, 'wrld');
  ser.Value("orientation", orientation, 'ori0');
}
```

> The usage of the `eid` compression policy, is to be taken care of which makes sure that `entityId` points to the same entity. Refer to the *Network identifiers* section in this chapter for more information on why the policy is required.

Now that we have defined our RMI parameters, we'll need to declare two RMIs: one for the client and one for the server:

```
DECLARE_SERVER_RMI_NOATTACH(SvRequestMoveEntity,
  SMoveEntityParams, eNRT_ReliableUnordered);


DECLARE_CLIENT_RMI_NOATTACH(ClMoveEntity, SMoveEntityParams,
  eNRT_ReliableUnordered);
```

All that's left now is for us to create the function implementations, which we can do in our CPP file by using the `IMPLEMENT_RMI` macro:

```
IMPLEMENT_RMI(CGameRules, SvRequestMoveEntity)
{
  IEntity *pEntity = gEnv->pEntitySystem-
    >GetEntity(params.entityId);
  if(pEntity == nullptr)
    return true;

  pEntity->SetWorldTM(Matrix34::Create(Vec3(1, 1, 1),
    params.orientation, params.position));

  GetGameObject()->InvokeRMI(ClMoveEntity(), params,
    eRMI_ToAllClients | eRMI_NoLocalCalls);

  return true;
}
```

This code defines our `SvRequestMoveEntity` function, which will be called when a client does the following:

```
GetGameObject()->InvokeRMI(SvRequestMoveEntity(), params,
    eRMI_Server);
```

Try to implement the `ClMoveEntity` function on your own. It should set the world transformation (`IEntity::SetWorldTM`) of the entity in the same manner as we did in `SvRequestMoveEntity`.

Network aspect serialization

Game object extensions can implement the `IGameObjectExtension::NetSerialize` function, which is called to serialize data relevant to the extension across the network.

Aspects

To allow separation of data relevant to specific mechanics, the net serialization process exposes **Aspects**. When an aspect is declared as "dirty" (changed) on the server or a client, the network will trigger this for serialization and call the `NetSerialize` function with the specific aspect.

To mark your aspect as dirty, call `IGameObject::ChangedNetworkState`:

```
GetGameObject()->ChangedNetworkState(eEA_GameClientF);
```

This will trigger `NetSerialize` to serialize your aspect, and send its data to the remote machine(s) which will then be deserialized in the same function.

 An aspect is considered "dirty" when its value has changed from what was last sent to remote client or server.

For example, if we want to serialize a set of flags relevant to player input, we'll create a new aspect and mark it as dirty whenever the input flags changes on the client:

```
bool CMyGameObjectExtension::NetSerialize(TSerialize ser,
    EEntityAspects aspect, uint8 profile, int flags)
{
  switch(aspect)
  {
    case eEA_GameClientF:
      {
        ser.EnumValue("inputFlags", (EInputFlags &)m_inputFlags,
          EInputFlag_First, EInputFlag_Last);
      }
```

```
        break;
    }
}
```

TSerialize::EnumValue is a specialized form of TSerialize::Value which calculates the minimum and maximum value of the enum, effectively functioning as a dynamic compression policy.

EnumValue and compression policies should be used wherever possible, in order to reduce bandwidth usage.

Now, when the eEA_GameClientF aspect is marked as dirty on the client, the NetSerialize function will be called and will write the m_inputFlags variable value to the network.

When the data arrives on the remote client or server, the NetSerialize function will once again be called, but this time writes the value to the m_inputFlags variable so that the server is aware of the new input flags provided by the client.

Aspects cannot support conditional serialization, and therefore each aspect has to serialize the same variables on each run. For example, if you serialized four floats during the first aspect serialization, you will always have to serialize four floats.

It's still possible to serialize complex objects, for example, we could write the length of an array and then iterate over it to read/write each object contained within the array.

Compression policies

TSerialize::Value enables the ability to pass an additional parameter, the compression policy. This policy is used to determine what compression mechanics can be used to optimize network bandwidth when synchronizing the data.

The compression policies are defined in Scripts/Network/CompressionPolicy.xml. Examples of existing policies can be seen as follows:

- eid: This is used when serializing the entityId identifiers across the network, and compares the game object's SNetObjectID to obtain the correct entityId on the remote client.

- wrld: This is used when serializing a Vec3 struct that represents world coordinates. This may have to be tweaked for bigger levels, due to being capped at 4095 by default.

- colr: This is used to serialize a ColorF struct across the network, allowing a floating point variable to represent values between 0 and 1.

- bool: This is a specific implementation for Boolean, and cuts down on a lot of bloat data.

- ori1: This is used to serialize the Quat structs over the network, for player orientation.

Creating a new compression policy

Adding new compression policies is as easy as modifying CompressionPolicy.xml. For example, if we want to create a new Vec3 policy in which the X and Y axes can only reach up to 2048 m, while the Z axis is limited to 1024 m:

```
<Policy name="wrld2" impl="QuantizedVec3">
  <XParams min="0" max="2047.0" nbits="24"/>
  YParams min="0" max="2047.0" nbits="24"/>
  <ZParams min="0" max="1023.0" nbits="24"/>
</Policy>
```

Exposing Lua entities to the network

Now that we know how to handle network communication in C++, let's have a look at how we can expose Lua entities to the network.

Net.Expose

In order to define RMIs and server properties, we'll need to call Net.Expose from within the global scope of your .lua script:

```
Net.Expose({
  Class = MyEntity,
  ClientMethods = {
    ClRevive              = { RELIABLE_ORDERED, POST_ATTACH,
      ENTITYID, },
  },
  ServerMethods = {
    SvRequestRevive       = { RELIABLE_UNORDERED, POST_ATTACH,
      ENTITYID, },
  },
  ServerProperties = {
  },
});
```

The previous function will define the `ClRevive` and `SvRequestRevive` RMIs, which can be called by using three subtables that are automatically created for your entity:

- `allClients`
- `otherClients`
- `server`

Function implementation

The remote functions are defined within either the `Client` or `Server` subtables of your entity script, so that the networking system can quickly find them while avoiding name conflicts.

For example, see the following `SvRequestRevive` function:

```
function MyEntity.Server:SvRequestRevive(playerEntityId)
end
```

Invoking RMIs

On the server, we can trigger the `ClRevive` function on all remote clients, along with the parameter that we defined previously.

On the server

To invoke our `SvRequestRevive` function on the server, simply use:

```
self.server:SvRequestRevive(playerEntityId);
```

On all clients

If you want all clients to receive a `ClRevive` call:

```
self.allClients:ClRevive(playerEntityId);
```

On all other clients

To send the `ClRevive` call to all clients except the current one:

```
self.otherClients:ClRevive(playerEntityId);
```

Binding our entity to the network

Prior to being able to send and receive RMI's, we'll have to bind our entity to the network. This is done by creating a game object for our entity:

```
CryAction.CreateGameObjectForEntity(self.id);
```

Our entity will now have a functional game object, but it's not yet set up for networked usage. To enable this, call the `CryAction.BindGameObjectToNetwork` function:

```
CryAction.BindGameObjectToNetwork(self.id);
```

Done! Our entity is now bound to the network, and can send and receive RMI's. Note that this should be immediately after the entity is spawned.

Summary

In this chapter, we have learned how CryENGINE instances can communicate with each other remotely over networks, and have also created our own RMI function.

You should now be aware of network aspects and compression policies function, and have basic knowledge of how you can expose entities to the network.

If you would like to proceed with multiplayer games and networking before moving on to the next chapter, why not create a basic multiplayer sample in which players can send a spawn request to the server that results in the player spawning on all remote clients?

In the next chapter, we'll be covering the physics system and how it can be used to your advantage.

9
Physics Programming

The CryENGINE physics system is an extensible physics implementation that allows for the creation of a truly dynamic world. With a sizeable API, developers will find that there's plenty of wiggle room when it comes to implementing physical simulations.

In this chapter, we will:

- Learn the workings of the physics system
- Discover how to debug our physicalized geometry
- Learn how to ray cast and intersect primitives to discover contact points, ground normal, and more
- Create our own physicalized entity
- Make things go boom by using simulated explosions

CryPhysics

The physical entity system is oriented around the concepts of physical entities, which are accessible via the `IPhysicalEntity` interface. A physical entity represents geometry with a physical proxy that can affect and be affected by intersections, collisions, and other events.

Although it is possible to create physical entities without an underlying entity (`IEntity`) via the `IPhysicalWorld::CreatePhysicalEntity` function, it is most common to call `IEntity::Physicalize` in order to enable the physics proxy of the model currently loaded by the entity.

 The physics proxy is a simplified model of the render mesh. This is used to decrease the strain on the physics system.

When `IEntity::Physicalize` is called, a new entity proxy is created that will handle its physicalized representation via a call to `IPhysicalWorld::CreatePhy sicalEntity`. The CryENGINE allows for a number of physical entity types to be created, depending on the purpose of the physicalized object.

Physicalized entity types

Following are the types of physicalized entities currently implemented by the CryENGINE:

- **PE_NONE**: This is used when the entity should not be physicalized, or passed to `IEntity::Physicalize` when we want to dephysicalize. While not physicalized, the entity will not have a physics proxy and can therefore not physically interact with other objects.

- **PE_STATIC**: This tells the physics system to utilize the entity's physics proxy, but never allows it to be moved or rotated through the use of physical interactions.

- **PE_RIGID**: This applies the rigid body type to the object, which allows foreign objects to collide and move the target.

- **PE_WHEELEDVEHICLE**: This is a specialized type used for vehicles.

- **PE_LIVING**: This is used for living actors, such as humans, that require ground alignment and ground contact queries.

- **PE_PARTICLE**: This physicalizes based on the particle passed in `SEntityPhysicalizeParams`, and is useful for avoiding issues with fast moving objects such as projectiles.

- **PE_ARTICULATED**: This is used for articulated structures consisting of several rigid bodies connected by joints, and is used on, for example, ragdolls.

- **PE_ROPE**: This is used for creating physicalized rope objects that can tie together two physical entities, or hang freely. It is also used for the Sandbox rope tool.

- **PE_SOFT**: This is a a collection of connected vertices that can interact with the environment, for example, cloth.

Introducing physical entity identifiers

All physical entities are assigned unique identifiers which can be retrieved via `IPhys` `icalWorld::GetPhysicalEntityId`, and used to obtain the physical entity via `IPhy` `sicalWorld::GetPhysicalEntityById`.

 The physical entity ID is serialized as a way to associate data with specific physical entities, and should therefore be consistent between reloads.

Drawing entity proxies

We can make use of the `p_draw_helpers` CVar to get visual feedback on the various physicalized objects present in the level.

To draw all physicalized objects, simply set the CVar to 1.

For more complex usage, use `p_draw_helpers [Entity_Types]_[Helper_Types]`.

For example, to draw the terrain proxy geometry:

```
p_draw_helpers t_g
```

Entity types

Following is a list of entity types:

- **t**: This shows terrain
- **s**: This shows static entities
- **r**: This shows sleeping rigid bodies
- **R**: This shows active rigid bodies
- **l**: This shows living entities
- **i**: This shows independent entities
- **g**: This shows triggers
- **a**: This shows areas
- **y**: This shows the `RayWorldIntersection` rays
- **e**: This shows explosion occlusion maps

Helper types

Following is a list of helper types:

- **g**: This shows geometry
- **c**: This shows contact points
- **b**: This shows bounding boxes
- **l**: This shows tetrahedral lattices for breakable objects
- **j**: This shows structural joints (will force translucency on the main geometry)
- **t(#)**: This shows bounding volume trees up to the level #
- **f(#)**: This only shows geometries with this bit flag set (multiple f's stack)

Physical entity actions, parameters, and status

The `IPhysicalEntity` interface provides three methods of altering and obtaining the physical state of the entity:

Parameters

Physical entity parameters determine how the physical representation of the geometry should behave in the world. Parameters can be retrieved via the `IPhysicalEntity::GetParams` function, and set by using `IPhysicalEntity::SetParams`.

All parameters are passed as structs that derive from `pe_params`. For example, to modify what gravity the entity is affected by, we can use `pe_simulation_params`:

```
pe_simulation_params simParams;

simParams.gravity = Vec3(0, 0, -9.81f);
GetEntity()->GetPhysics()->SetParams(&simParams);
```

This code will change the gravitational pull that is applied to the entity to -9.81f.

 Most of the physical entity parameter struct's default constructors mark certain data as unused; this way we don't have to worry about overriding parameters we did not set.

Actions

Similar in usage to parameters, actions allow the developer to force certain physical events, such as impulses or resetting entity velocity.

All actions are derived from the `pe_action` struct, and can be applied via the `IPhysicalEntity::Action` function.

For example, to apply a simple impulse to our entity which launches it into the air, use:

```
pe_action_impulse impulseAction;
impulseAction.impulse = Vec3(0, 0, 10);

GetEntity()->GetPhysics()->Action(&impulseAction);
```

Status

It is also possible to get various status data from the entity, to, for example, determine where its center of mass is, or to get its velocity.

All statuses are derived from the `pe_status` struct, and can be retrieved via the `IPhysicalEntity::GetStatus` function.

For example, to get the velocity of a living physical entity such as a player, use:

```
pe_status_living livStat;
GetEntity()->GetPhysics()->GetStatus(&livStat);

Vec3 velocity = livStat.vel;
```

Physicalized entity type details

There are a number of parameters, actions, and statuses for the default physicalized entity implementation. We have listed a selection of their most commonly used types:

Common parameters

- **pe_params_pos**: This is used to set the position and orientation of the physical entity.
- **pe_params_bbox**: This allows forcing an entity's bounding box to a specific value, or querying it when used with `GetParams`, as well as querying intersections.

- **pe_params_outer_entity**: This allows specifying an outer physical entity. Collisions with the outer entity will be ignored if they occur within the bounding box of it.
- **pe_simulation_params**: This sets simulation parameters for compatible entities.

Common actions

- **pe_action_impulse**: This applies a one-time impulse to the entity.
- **pe_action_add_constraint**: This is used to add a constraint between two physical entities. For example, an ignore constraint could be used to make a ghost walk through walls.
- **pe_action_set_velocity**: This is used to force the velocity of a physical entity.

Common statuses

- **pe_status_pos**: This requests the current transformation of an entity or an entity part
- **pe_status_dynamics**: This is used to get entity movement stats such as acceleration, angular acceleration, and velocity

Static

Physicalizing an entity with the static type results in the creation of the base physicalized entity type, from which all extensions such as rigid or living are derived.

Static entities are physicalized, but will not move. For example, if a ball is thrown at a static object, it will bounce back without moving the target object.

Rigid

This refers to basic physicalized entity that can be moved in the world when affected by external forces.

If we use the same previous example, throwing a ball at a rigid object will result in the rigid object being pushed away

Wheeled vehicle

This represents a wheeled vehicle, putting it simply, the implementation is a rigid body with added vehicle functionality such as wheels, brakes, and the CryENGINE.

Unique parameters

- **pe_params_car**: This is used to get or set vehicle-specific parameters, such as CryENGINE power, RPM, and the number of gears
- **pe_params_wheel**: This is used to get or set parameters specific to one of the vehicle's wheels, such as friction, surface ID, and damping

Unique statuses

- **pe_status_vehicle**: This is used to get vehicle stats, allows getting velocity, current gear, and more
- **pe_status_wheel**: This gets the status of a specific wheel, for example, contact normal, torque, and surface ID
- **pe_status_vehicle_abilities**: This allows checking of the maximum possible velocity for a specific turn

Unique actions

- **pe_action_drive**: This is used on vehicle events such as brakes, pedals, and gear switches.

Living

The living entity implementation is a specialized setup for handling actors and their movement requests.

Living entities have two states: on ground and in air. When on ground, the player will be "glued" to the ground until an attempt to detach it is made (by applying significant velocity away from the ground).

 Remember the animated character movement requests from *Chapter 5, Creating Custom Actors*? The system uses living entity pe_action_move requests in the core.

Unique parameters

- **pe_player_dimensions**: This is used to set parameters related to the living entity's static properties, such as sizeCollider, and whether it should use a capsule or cylinder for the collision geometry

- **pe_player_dynamics**: This is used to set dynamic parameters related to the living entity, such as inertia, gravity, and mass

Unique statuses

- **pe_status_living**: This gets the current living entity status, including stats such as time flying, velocity, and ground normal

- **pe_status_check_stance**: This is used to check whether new dimensions cause collisions. Parameters have the same meaning as in pe_player_dimensions

Unique actions

- **pe_action_move**: This is used to submit move requests for the entity.

Particle

It is also possible to use particle representations of objects. This is commonly done for objects that should move at high speeds, for example, projectiles. Essentially, this means that the physics representation of our entity is simply a two-dimensional plane.

Unique parameters

- **pe_params_particle**: This is used to set particle-specific parameters

Articulated

Articulated structures consist of several rigid bodies connected by joints, for example, a ragdoll. This approach allows for setting tearing limits and more.

Unique parameters

- **pe_params_joint**: This is used to create a joint between two rigid bodies when setting, and queries an existing joint when used together with `GetParams`.

- **pe_params_articulated_body**: This is used to set parameters specific to the articulated type.

Rope

When you want to create ropes that tie multiple physicalized objects together, you should utilize ropes. This system allows ropes to attach to dynamic or static surfaces.

Unique parameters

- **pe_params_rope**: This is used to alter or get physics rope parameters

Soft

Soft is a system of non-rigidly connected vertices that can interact with the environment, for example, cloth objects.

Unique parameters

- **pe_params_softbody**: This is used to configure a physicalized soft body

Unique actions

- **pe_action_attach_points**: This is used to attach some of the soft entity's vertices to another physical entity

Ray world intersections

Using the `IPhysicalWorld::RayWorldIntersection` function, we can cast a ray from one point of our world to another to detect distance to specific objects, surface types, normal of ground, and more.

`RayWorldIntersection` is pretty easy to use, and we can prove it! To start off, see the following example of a ray cast:

```
ray_hit hit;

Vec3 origin = pEntity->GetWorldPos();
Vec3 dir = Vec3(0, 0, -1);

int numHits = gEnv->pPhysicalWorld->RayWorldIntersection(origin,
  dir, ent_static | ent_terrain, rwi_stop_at_pierceable |
    rwi_colltype_any, &hit, 1);
if(numHits > 0)
{
  // Hit something!
}
```

The ray_hit struct

A reference to our `ray_hit hit` variable is passed to `RayWorldIntersection`, and is where we'll be able to retrieve all of the information about the ray hit.

Commonly used member variables

- **float dist**: This is the distance from the origin (in our case the position of our entity) to the place where the ray hit.

- **IPhysicalEntity *pCollider**: This is the pointer to the physical entity that our ray collided with.

- **short surface_idx**: This is the surface identifier of the surface type of the material our ray collided with (see `IMaterialManager::GetSurfaceType` to get its `ISurfaceType` pointer).

- **Vec3 pt**: This is the point of contact, in world coordinates.

- **Vec3 n**: This is the surface normal at the point of contact.

- **ray_hit *next**: This points to the next `ray_hit` structure if our ray hit multiple times. See the *Allowing multiple ray hits* section for more information.

Origin and direction

The first and second parameters of the `RayWorldIntersection` function define from where the ray should be cast, and how far in a specific direction.

In our case, we shoot the ray from the current position of our entity, one unit downwards.

Object types and ray flags

Notice how after `dir`, we passed two types of flags to the `RayWorldIntersection` function. These indicate how the ray should intersect objects, and which collisions to ignore.

Object types

The object types parameter expects flags based on the `entity_query_flags` enum, and is used to determine what types of objects we want to allow our ray to collide with. If the ray collides with an object type that we did not define, it will simply ignore it and pass through.

- **ent_static**: This refers to static objects
- **ent_sleeping_rigid**: This indicates sleeping rigid bodies
- **ent_rigid**: This indicates active rigid bodies
- **ent_living**: This refers to living objects, for example, players
- **ent_independent**: This indicates independent objects
- **ent_terrain**: This indicates terrain
- **ent_all**: This refers to all types of objects

Ray flags

The ray flags parameter is based on the `rwi_flags` enum, and is used to determine how the cast should behave.

Allowing multiple ray hits

As mentioned earlier, it's also possible to allow the ray to hit objects multiple times. To do so, we simply create a `ray_hit` array and pass it to the `RayWorldIntersection` function along with the number of hits:

```
const int maxHits = 10;

ray_hit rayHits[maxHits];
int numHits = gEnv->pPhysicalWorld->RayWorldIntersection(origin,
  direction, ent_all, rwi_stop_at_pierceable, rayHits, maxHits);

for(int i = 0; i < numHits; i++)
{
  ray_hit *pRayHit = &rayHits[i];

// Process ray
}
```

Creating a physicalized entity

Now that we know how the physics system works, we can create our own physicalized entity that can collide with other physicalized geometry in our scene:

 This section assumes that you have read *Chapter 3, Creating and Utilizing Custom Entities*.

In C++

Based on what we learned earlier, we know that we can physicalize a static entity via the `PE_STATIC` type:

```
SEntityPhysicalizeParams physicalizeParams;
physicalizeParams.type = PE_STATIC;

pEntity->Physicalize(physicalizeParams);
```

Assuming that geometry had been loaded for the entity prior to calling `IEntity::Physicalize`, other physicalized objects will now be able to collide with our entity.

But what if we want to allow collisions to move our object in the world? That's where the `PE_RIGID` type comes into play:

```
SEntityPhysicalizeParams physicalizeParams;
physicalizeParams.type = PE_RIGID;
physicalizeParams.mass = 10;

pEntity->Physicalize(physicalizeParams);
```

Now, CryENGINE will know that our object weighs 10 kilograms, and will be moved when it collides with another physicalized entity.

In C#

We can also do this in C#, by using the `EntityBase.Physicalize` function, along with the `PhysicalizationParams` struct. For example, if we want to physicalize a static object, we would use the following code:

```
var physType = PhysicalizationType.Static;
var physParams = new PhysicalizationParams(physType);

Physicalize(physParams);
```

Of course, this assumes that an object has been loaded via the `EntityBase.LoadObject` method.

Now, if we want to make a rigid entity, we can use:

```
var physType = PhysicalizationType.Rigid;

var physParams = new PhysicalizationParams(physType);
physParams.mass = 50;

Physicalize(physParams);
```

Our entity now weighs 50 kilograms and can be moved when collisions with other physicalized objects occur.

Simulating explosions

We know you're thinking, "What good is all this physics knowledge if we can't blow stuff up?", and we've got you covered!

The physical world implementation provides a simple function for simulating explosions in the world, with a wide range of parameters to allow customization of the blast area.

To demonstrate, we'll create an explosion with a maximum radius of 100:

```
pe_explosion explosion;
explosion.rmax = 100;

gEnv->pPhysicalWorld->SimulateExplosion(&explosion);
```

The `SimulateExplosion` function will merely simulate an explosion and generate a force that pushes entities away, it will not create any particle effects.

Summary

In this chapter, we have learned the basic workings of the physical world implementation and how to visually debug physics proxies.

With your new knowledge, you should be aware of how you can use ray world intersections to gather knowledge about the surrounding game world. Oh, and we've blown stuff up.

If you don't feel ready to move on, why not create an extended physicalized entity or physics modifier such as a gravity gun, or a trampoline?

In the next chapter, we'll be covering the rendering pipeline, including how to author custom shaders, and how to modify materials at runtime.

10
Rendering Programming

The CryENGINE renderer is most likely the most well-known part of the engine, providing highly complex graphical features with great performance on platforms such as PC, Xbox 360, and PlayStation 3.

In this chapter we will cover the following topics:

- Learning the basic workings of the renderer
- Seeing how each frame is rendered to the world
- Learning the basics of shader authoring
- Learning how it's possible to modify static objects at runtime
- Modifying a material at runtime

The renderer details

The CryENGINE renderer is a modular system that allows the drawing of complex scenes, the handling of shaders, and more.

In order to facilitate different platform architectures, there exist multiple renderers for CryENGINE, all implementing the **IRenderer** interface. We have listed a selection as shown:

- DirectX: Used on Windows and Xbox
- PSGL: Used on PlayStation 3

There is also most likely an **OpenGL** renderer in development, for use on platforms such as Linux and Mac OS X.

Shaders

Shaders in CryENGINE are written using a specialized language based on HLSL, called CryFX. The system is very similar to HLSL, but is specialized for core engine functionality such as material and shader parameters, `#include` macros, and more.

 Note that shader authoring was not enabled in the Free SDK at the time this book was written; however, this might change in the future.

Shader permutations

Each time a material alters a shader generation parameter, a permutation of the base shader will be created. The engine also exposes functionality for exposing engine variables to shaders, to disable or tweak effects at runtime.

This is possible due to the CryFX language allowing the `#ifdef`, `#endif`, and `#include` blocks, allowing the engine to strip certain parts of the shader code out at runtime.

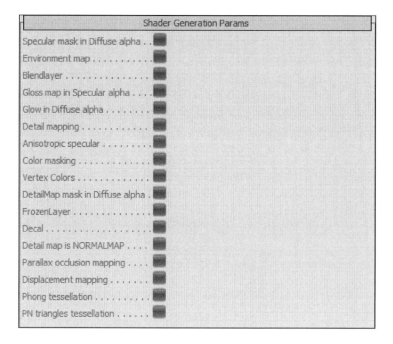

Shader cache

Since compiling shaders at runtime is not viable on all platforms, CryENGINE provides the shader caching system. This allows for the storage of a collection of precompiled shaders, sparing quite a bit of work for the end-user's device.

 As mentioned in the previous section, shaders can contain a huge amount of variations of themselves. Therefore, it is necessary to make sure that all required permutations have been compiled when setting up the cache.

PAK files

The renderer can load four .pak files from the Engine folder, containing shader definitions, source files, and more.

Archive name	Description
Shaders.pak	Contains shader source files and .ext (definition) files. Shader source is commonly excluded from this archive when using precompiled shader cache.
ShadersBin.pak	Contains binary parsed information of the shader source code.
ShaderCache.pak	Contains all compiled shaders; used only when the shader cannot be found in the current level's shader cache.
ShaderCacheStartup.pak	Loaded during startup to speed up boot times; should only contain shaders that are required for the main menu.

Render nodes

The **IRenderNode** interface is provided in order to provide the Cry3DEngine system with a way to manage objects.

This allows for generating object visibility hierarchies (allowing an easy method of culling objects that are not currently seen) and rendering of the object.

Rendering breakdown

The rendering of games is divided into two steps:

1. Pre update
2. Post update

Pre update

The initial step in rendering each frame to the scene occurs in the IGameFramework::PreUpdate function. Pre update is responsible for updating most game systems (such as flowgraph, view system, and more) and makes the initial call to ISystem::RenderBegin.

 PreUpdate is most commonly called from CGame::Update, in the stock CryGame.dll. Always keep in mind that this process only applies to the Launcher application; the Editor handles game updates and rendering uniquely.

RenderBegin signals the start of a new frame, and tells the renderer to set the new frame ID, clear buffers, and more.

Post update

After updating the game systems, it's time to render the scene. This initial step is done via the IGameFramework::PostUpdate function.

Prior to rendering, systems that are crucial to the new information retrieved from the game update done within and after PreUpdate must be updated. This includes flash UI, animation synching, and more.

After that is done, PostUpdate will call ISystem::Render, which in turn renders the world using the I3DEngine::RenderWorld function.

After rendering the world, the system will call functions such as IFlashUI::Update, and PostUpdate on all game objects, and more, finally ending in a call to ISystem::RenderEnd.

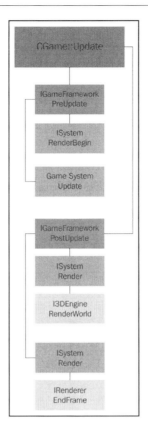

Rendering new viewports using render contexts

Render contexts are in essence wrappers for native window handles. On Windows, this allows you to specify a **HWND**, and then have the renderer draw directly to it.

The very nature of render contexts is platform-specific, and is, therefore, not guaranteed to work the same from one rendering module (such as, D3D) to another (such as, OpenGL).

Note: Render contexts are currently only supported while running in Editor mode on Windows, which is used for rendering viewports in tool windows.

In order to create a new context with your window handle, call
`IRenderer::CreateContext`.

 Note that contexts are automatically enabled on creation; call `IRenderer` `::MakeMainContextActive` to re-enable the main view.

Rendering

When rendering a context, the first thing you need to do is activate it. This can be done by using `IRenderer::SetCurrentContext`. Once enabled, the renderer is aware of the window that it should be passing to DirectX.

The next thing you need to do is update the resolution of the context by using `IRenderer::ChangeViewport`. This instructs the renderer about the position and size of the area it should render.

After doing so, simply call the typical render functions such as `IRenderer::BeginFrame` (see the *Rendering breakdown* section), and then finish by making the main context active at the end, via `IRenderer::MakeMainContextActive`.

Using the I3DEngine::RenderWorld function

In some cases it might make sense to call `I3DEngine::RenderWorld` manually instead of relying on the game framework's update process.

To do so, we'll need to change the process a bit. To start, call `IRenderer::SetCurrentContext` followed by `IRenderer::MakeMainContextActive` as shown:

```
gEnv->pRenderer->SetCurrentContext(hWnd);
// Restore context
gEnv->pRenderer->MakeMainContextActive();
```

Good, now our context will be activated. But in order to actually render, we'll need to fill up the void between. To start, we have to call `IRenderer::ChangeViewport` directly after `SetCurrentContext` as shown:

```
gEnv->pRenderer->ChangeViewport(0, 0, width, height, true);
```

This sets the viewport to the coordinates of `0`, `0`, and our specified `width` and `height` variables.

After setting the viewport size, you'll want to configure your camera to the new resolution and call `IRenderer::SetCamera` as shown:

```
CCamera camera;
// Set frustrum based on width, height and field of view (60)
camera.SetFrustum(width, height, DEG2RAD(60));
// Set camera scale, orientation and position.
Vec3 scale(1, 1, 1);
Quat rotation = Quat::CreateRotationXYZ(Ang3(DEG2RAD(-45), 0, 0));
Vec3 position(0, 0, 0);
camera.SetMatrix(Matrix34::Create(scale, rotation, position));
gEnv->pRenderer->SetCamera(m_camera);
```

Great! The renderer is now aware of which camera it should use for rendering. We'll also need to supply this to `I3DEngine::RenderWorld` later on. But first we have to clear the buffers in order to remove the previous frame with the following code:

```
// Set clear color to pure black
ColorF clearColor(0.f)

gEnv->pRenderer->SetClearColor(Vec3(clearColor.r, clearColor.g,
    clearColor.b));
gEnv->pRenderer->ClearBuffer(FRT_CLEAR, &clearColor);
```

This is then followed by calling `IRenderer::RenderBegin` to indicate that it's time to start rendering:

```
gEnv->pSystem->RenderBegin();
gEnv->pSystem->SetViewCamera(m_camera);

// Insert rendering here

gEnv->pSystem->RenderEnd();
```

Now all we have to do is render the scene between the `SetViewCamera` and `RenderEnd` calls:

```
gEnv->pRenderer->SetViewport(0, 0, width, height);
gEnv->p3DEngine->Update();

int renderFlags = SHDF_ALLOW_AO | SHDF_ALLOWPOSTPROCESS |
    SHDF_ALLOW_WATER | SHDF_ALLOWHDR | SHDF_ZPASS;

gEnv->p3DEngine->RenderWorld(renderFlags, &camera, 1,
    __FUNCTION__);
```

Done! The world is now rendered based on our camera setup, and should be visible to you in the window set via `IRenderer::SetCurrentContext`.

I3DEngine::RenderWorld flags

The render flags determine how the world should be drawn. For example, we could exclude `SHDF_ALLOW_WATER` to completely avoid rendering water. The following table lists the available flags and their function:

Flag name	Description
SHDF_ALLOWHDR	If not set, HDR will not be used.
SHDF_ZPASS	Allows the Z-Pass.
SHDF_ZPASS_ONLY	Allows the Z-Pass, and no other passes.
SHDF_DO_NOT_CLEAR_Z_BUFFER	If set, the Z-buffer will never be cleared.
SHDF_ALLOWPOSTPROCESS	If not set, all post-process effects will be ignored.
SHDF_ALLOW_AO	If set, **Ambient Occlusion** will be used.
SHDF_ALLOW_WATER	If not set, all water will be ignored and not rendered.
SHDF_NOASYNC	No asynchronous drawing.
SHDF_NO_DRAWNEAR	Excludes all rendering in the near plane.
SHDF_STREAM_SYNC	Enables synchronized texture streaming.
SHDF_NO_DRAWCAUSTICS	If set, no water caustics will be drawn.

Shaders

Creating a custom shader in CryENGINE is relatively easy, and can be done simply by copying an existing shader (`.cfx`) and its extension file (`.ext`). For the sake of this example, copy `Illum.ext` from `Engine/Shaders` and name it `MyShader.ext`. Then copy `Engine/Shaders/HWScripts/CryFX/Illum.cfx` and rename it to `MyShader.cfx`.

Note that creating custom shaders should be thought out properly; if it is possible to simply use an existing shader, that would be the best option. This is due to the fact that CryENGINE is already reaching the viable limit of the number of shader permutations.

 As stated earlier in the chapter, custom shader authoring was not enabled in the CryENGINE Free SDK at the time this book was written.

The shader description

Each shader needs to define a description, which sets its options. Options are set in the global `Script` variable, as shown in the following code:

```
float Script : STANDARDSGLOBAL
<
  string Script =
          "Public;"
          "SupportsDeferredShading;"
          "SupportsAttrInstancing;"
          "ShaderDrawType = Light;"
          "ShaderType = General;"
>;
```

Texture slots

Each material can specify the file path to a texture in a set of texture slots as shown:

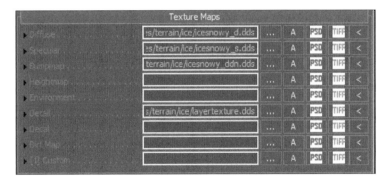

We can access these texture slots via shaders by using a set of helpers (as follows), which can then be added to custom samplers that can then be loaded by using the `GetTexture2D` function.

Slot name	Helper name
Diffuse	$Diffuse
Gloss (Specular)	$Gloss
Bump	
Bump heightmap	$BumpHeight
Environment	$Env
Environment Cubemap	$EnvironmentCubeMap
Detail	$Detail

Slot name	Helper name
Opacity	$Opacity
Decal	$DecalOverlay
Subsurface	$Subsurface
Custom	$CustomMap
Custom Secondary	$CustomSecondaryMap

Shader flags

By using the `#ifdef` and `#endif` preprocessor commands, it is possible to define areas of the code that can be removed prior to compilation or at runtime. This allows for the usage of a single übershader with multiple toggleable subeffects, such as Illum.

For example, we could check whether the user is running DX11 as follows:

```
#if D3D11
// Include DX11 specific shader code here
#endif
```

Material flags

Material flags are set via **Material Editor**, allowing each material to use different effects, such as Parallax Occlusion Mapping and Tessellation. The material flags are evaluated at compile time.

To create a new material flag, open your shader's `.ext` file and create a new property with the following code:

```
Property
{
  Name = %MYPROPERTY
  Mask = 0x160000000
  Property    (My Property)
  Description (My property is a very good property)
}
```

Now when you restart the editor, your property should appear in the Material Editor.

The following is a list of possible property data:

Property data	Description
Name	Defines the internal name of the property, and is what you should check for by using the `#ifdef` block.
Mask	Unique mask used to identify your property. Should not conflict with that of other properties in your shader definition (`.ext`).
Property	The public name of the property, displayed in the material editor.
Description	Public description for the property, shown when hovering over the property in the material editor.
DependencySet	When the user modifies the value of the texture slot this property is set to, the material flag will be activated.
	This is most commonly used in combination with the Hidden flag.
DependencyReset	When the user modifies the value of the texture slot this property is set to, the material flag will be cleared.
	Used to avoid conflicts with other material flags.
Hidden	If set, the property will not be visible in the editor.

Engine flags

Engine flags are directly set by the engine, and contain information such as the currently supported shader model or the platform on which the engine is currently running.

Runtime flags

Runtime flags are defined by the `%_RT_` prefix, and can be set or unset by the engine at runtime. All available flags can be viewed in the `RunTime.ext` file.

Samplers

A sampler is a representation of a single texture of a specific texture type. By creating custom samplers, we can refer to specific textures from within the shader, for example, to load a texture containing pre-generated noise.

An example for a pre-loaded sampler is as shown in the following code:

```
sampler2D mySampler = sampler_state
{
  Texture = EngineAssets/Textures/myTexture.dds;
  MinFilter = LINEAR;
  MagFilter = LINEAR;
  MipFilter = LINEAR;
  AddressU = Wrap;
  AddressV = Wrap;
  AddressW = Wrap;
}
```

We can now refer to `mySampler` in our code.

Using texture slots with samplers

In some cases, it's preferred to have your sampler point to one of the texture slots defined in the material.

To do so, simply replace the path of your texture with the name of your preferred texture slot:

```
sampler2D mySamplerWithTextureSlot = sampler_state
{
  Texture = $Diffuse;
  MinFilter = LINEAR;
  MagFilter = LINEAR;
  MipFilter = LINEAR;
  AddressU = Wrap;
  AddressV = Wrap;
  AddressW = Wrap;
}
```

When loaded, the texture will then be that which the material specified in the Diffuse slot.

Obtaining a texture

Now that we have a texture, we can learn how to get texture data in a shader. This is done by using the `GetTexture2D` function as shown:

```
half4 myMap = GetTexture2D(mySampler, baseTC.xy);
```

The first parameter specifies which sampler to use (in our case, the sampler we created previously), while the second specifies the texture coordinates.

Manipulating static objects at runtime

In this section we are going to learn how to modify a static mesh at runtime, allowing for the manipulation of render and physical meshes during gameplay.

To do this, firstly we need to obtain the `IStatObj` instance of our object. For example, if you're modifying an entity, you can use `IEntity::GetStatObj` as shown:

```
IStatObj *pStatObj = pMyEntity->GetStatObj(0);
```

Note that we passed 0 as the first parameter to `IEntity::GetStatObj`. This is done in order to get the object with the highest **Level of Detail** (**LOD**). This means that changes made to this static object will not be reflected in its other LODs.

You now have a pointer to an interface holding the static object data for your model.

We can now call `IStatObj::GetIndexedMesh` or `IStatObj::GetRenderMesh`. The latter is most likely the best place to start, as it is constructed from the optimized indexed mesh data as shown in the following code:

```
IIndexedMesh *pIndexedMesh = pStatObj->GetIndexedMesh();
if(pIndexedMesh)
{
  IIndexedMesh::SMeshDescription meshdesc;
  pIndexedMesh->GetMesh(meshdesc);
}
```

We now have access to the `meshdesc` variable containing information about the mesh.

Note that we need to call `IStatObj::UpdateVertices` in order to carry over the changes we have made to the mesh.

Remember that changing a static object will carry over the changes to all of the objects using it. Use the `IStatObj::Clone` method to create a copy of it prior to editing, allowing you to manipulate only one object in the scene.

Modifying materials at runtime

In this section we're going to modify a material at runtime.

 Similar to `IStatObj`, we can also clone our material to avoid making changes to all of the objects using it currently. To do so, call `IMaterialManager::CloneMaterial`, which is accessible via `gEnv->p3DEngine->GetMaterialManager()`.

The first thing we need to do is obtain an instance of the material we want to edit. If we have an entity nearby, we can use `IEntity::GetMaterial` as shown:

```
IMaterial *pMaterial = pEntity->GetMaterial();
```

 Note that `IEntity::GetMaterial` returns null if no custom material has been set. If this is the case, you might want to rely on a function such as `IStatObj::GetMaterial`.

Cloning a material

Note that `IMaterial` instances can be used for multiple objects. This means that modifying an object's parameters can result in changes on objects other than that you retrieved the object from.

To resolve this, we can simply clone the material before modifying it via the `IMaterialManager::Clone` method as shown:

```
IMaterial *pNewMaterial = gEnv->p3DEngine->GetMaterialManager()-
    >CloneMaterial(pMaterial);
```

Then we just have to apply the clone to the entity we retrieved the original instance from:

```
pEntity->SetMaterial(pNewMaterial);
```

We can now move on to modifying the material's parameters, or parameters related to the shader that was assigned to it.

Material parameters

Modifying the parameters of our material can be useful at times. This allows us to tweak per-material properties such as **Opacity**, **AlphaTest**, and **Diffuse Color** as shown in the following screenshot:

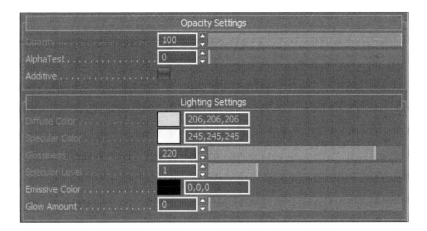

To set or get material parameters, use `IMaterial::SetGetMaterialParamFloat` or `IMaterial::SetGetMaterialVec3`.

For example, to see the alpha of our material, use the following code:

```
float newAlpha = 0.5f;
pMaterial->SetGetMaterialParamFloat("alpha",  0.5f, false);
```

The material should now draw alpha at half strength.

The following is a list of available parameters:

Parameter name	Type
"alpha"	float
"opacity"	float
"glow"	float
"shininess"	float
"diffuse"	Vec3
"emissive"	Vec3
"specular"	Vec3

Shader parameters

As we learned earlier, each shader can expose a set of parameters that allow the material to tweak the behavior of the shader without affecting the shader globally.

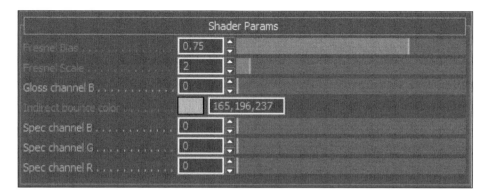

To modify the shader parameters of our material, we'll first need to obtain the shader item linked to this material:

```
const SShaderItem& shaderItem(pMaterial->GetShaderItem());
```

Now that we have the shader item, we can access `IRenderShaderResources::GetParameters` with the following code:

```
DynArray<SShaderParam> params = shaderItem.m_pShaderResources->GetParameters();
```

We can now modify the parameters contained within and call `IRenderShaderResources::SetShaderParams` as shown:

```
// Iterate through the parameters to find the one we want to
  modify
for(auto it = params.begin(), end = params.end(); it != end; ++it)
{
  SShaderParam param = *it;

  if(!strcmp(paramName, param.m_Name))
  {
    UParamVal paramVal;
    paramVal.m_Float = 0.7f;

    // Set the value of the parameter (to 0.7f in this case)
    param.SetParam(paramName, &params, paramVal);
```

```
SInputShaderResources res;
shaderItem.m_pShaderResources->ConvertToInputResource(&res);

res.m_ShaderParams = params;

// Update the parameters in the resources.
shaderItem.m_pShaderResources-
   >SetShaderParams(&res,shaderItem.m_pShader);
break;
   }
}
```

Example – Dynamic alpha-test for vegetation

Now let's put your knowledge to the test!

We have included a tree set up for use of the alpha test property with the sample (as shown in the following screenshot). When alpha test is increased, leaf loss is simulated.

To show this off, we're going to write a little snippet of code that modifies this at runtime.

Start by creating a new class, called CTreeOfTime. Either create a new game object extension, or derive one from the sample that we created in *Chapter 3, Creating and Utilizing Custom Entities*.

Once created, we'll need to load our tree object on entity spawn as shown:

```
void CTreeOfTime::ProcessEvent(SEntityEvent& event)
{
  switch(event.event)
  {
    case ENTITY_EVENT_INIT:
    case ENTITY_EVENT_RESET:
    case ENTITY_EVENT_START_LEVEL:
    {
      IEntity *pEntity = GetEntity();

      pEntity->LoadGeometry(0,
        "Objects/nature/trees/ash/tree_ash_01.cgf");
    }
    break;
  }
}
```

Our entity should now load the Objects/nature/trees/ash/tree_ash_01.cgf object into its first slot (Index 0) when it is spawned.

Next, we'll need to override the entities Update method in order to update the alpha-test property based on the current time of day. When you're done, add the following code:

```
if(IStatObj *pStatObj = GetEntity()->GetStatObj(0))
{
  IMaterial *pMaterial = pStatObj->GetMaterial();
  if(pMaterial == nullptr)
    return;

  IMaterial *pBranchMaterial = pMaterial->GetSubMtl(0);
  if(pBranchMaterial == nullptr)
    return;

  // Make alpha peak at 12
  float alphaTest = abs(gEnv->p3DEngine->GetTimeOfDay()->GetTime()
    - 12) / 12;
  pBranchMaterial->SetGetMaterialParamFloat("alpha", alphaTest,
    false);
}
```

You should now have a time cycle during which your tree loses and regains its leaves. This is one of the many techniques that are possible by modifying materials at runtime.

Summary

In this chapter, we have learned how shaders are used by the engine, and have broken down the rendering process. You should now be aware of how you can use render contexts, manipulate static objects at runtime, and modify materials progammatically.

If you aren't ready to move on to the next chapter on effects and sound just yet, why not take on a challenge? For example, you could create a custom object that is deformed when attacked.

11
Effects and Sound

CryENGINE hosts a very modular effects system, allowing the spawning of effects at runtime with minimal effort. The engine also features FMOD integration, giving the developer the tools for dynamic playback of audio, music, and localized dialogs.

In this chapter we will cover the following topics:

- Learning about the effects and sound systems
- Discovering how to create and trigger material effects
- Learning how to export and customize sounds via FMOD Designer
- Playing back custom sounds
- Learning how to integrate sounds into particles and physical events

Introducing effects

Without FX, the game world is usually hard to believe and is considered void of life. Simply adding effects such as sound and particles helps to make the world come alive, giving the player a much more immersive feeling of the world.

Although there isn't one combined system for all types of effects in the engine, we'll be covering a number of systems that handle effects of various sorts. This includes material effects, particle effects, sound effects, and more.

Material effects

The material effects system handles reactions between materials, for example, to play different particle and sound effects based on which material a rock lands on.

Surface types

Each material is assigned a **surface type**, indicating what type of surface it is. For example, if we are creating a rock material, we should use the mat_rock surface type.

By assigning a surface type, the physics system will be able to gather information on how collisions should behave, for example, by getting the surface type's friction value. Interactions between multiple surface types also allow for dynamic effects that change based on the surface types in contact with each other.

Surface types can be queried programmatically quite easily, allowing various systems to create different code paths that are triggered based on the surface type.

In C++, surface types are represented by the `ISurfaceType` interface, which can be obtained by using `IMaterial::GetSurfaceType`.

Using C#, surface types are represented by the `CryEngine.SurfaceType` class, and can be retrieved by using the `CryEngine.Material.SurfaceType` property.

Adding or modifying surface types

Surface types are defined in `Game/Libs/MaterialEffects/SurfaceTypes.xml`. The file is parsed by the engine at startup, allowing materials to use the loaded surface types.

Each surface type is defined by using the `SurfaceType` element, for example, `mat_fabric` as shown in the following code:

```
<SurfaceType name="mat_fabric">
  <Physics friction="0.80000001" elasticity="0" pierceability="7"
    can_shatter="1"/>
</SurfaceType>
```

The physics properties are queried by the physics system when collisions occur.

Particle effects

Particle effects are handled by the `IParticleManager` interface, accessible by using `I3DEngine::GetParticleManager`. To obtain a pointer to an `IParticleEffect` object, see `IParticleManager::FindEffect`.

Particle effects are created by using the **Particle Editor** contained in the **Sandbox Editor**, and are typically saved to `Game/Libs/Particles`.

Sound effects

The CryENGINE sound system is powered by FMOD, an audio content creation tool for games. By using FMOD, the engine supports easy creation and manipulation of sounds for immediate use in the game.

The sound system can be accessed via the `ISoundSystem` interface, which is commonly retrieved via the `gEnv->pSoundSystem` pointer. Sounds are represented by the `ISound` interface, from which a pointer can be retrieved via `ISoundSystem::CreateSound` or `ISoundSystem::GetSound`.

By accessing the `ISound` interface, we can alter semantics, distance multipliers, and more, as well as actually play the sound via `ISound::Play`.

FMOD Designer

The designer is what we'll use every time we want to add more sounds to the different sound libraries in use by our project.

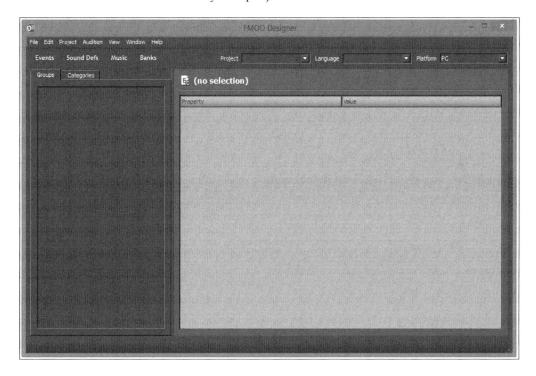

The designer allows the creation and maintenance of sound banks, essentially libraries that create a separation between different sounds. Within the sound banks are events, sound definitions, and music. These can be given static and dynamic modifiers, for example, to give distinctive 3D effects to the sounds depending on the in-game environment.

Creating and triggering material effects

There are two ways to trigger custom material effects, as explained in the following sections

Automated playback based on physical interactions

When two materials collide due to a physical event, the engine will look up a material effect in `Game/Libs/MaterialEffects/MaterialEffects.xml` based on the surface types assigned to the materials. This allows various particles and sounds to be played when certain interactions occur.

For example, if a rock collides with wood, we can play a specific sound event along with wood splinter particles.

To start, open `MaterialEffects.xml` with Microsoft Excel.

 Although it's possible to modify the material effects document manually, this is not recommended due to the complicated nature of the Excel format.

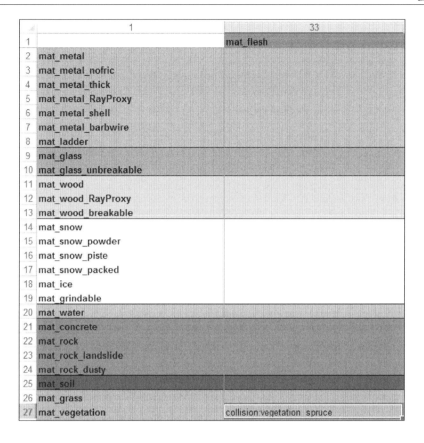

You should now see the material effects sheet inside your Excel application. The various surface types are laid out in a grid, and the intersection between the row and column defines which effect to use.

For example, judging by the sheet shown in the previous screenshot, if a material with the surface type **mat_flesh** collides with a **mat_vegetation** surface, the engine will load the **collision:vegetation_spruce** effect.

 A complete list of surface types can be viewed (or modified) via `Libs/MaterialEffects/SurfaceTypes.xml`.

Adding new surface types

If you need to add new surface types to the material effects document, simply add a corresponding row and a column with the surface type name, in order to have the engine load it.

 Remember that the names of your surface type must appear in the same order for both the row and column.

Effect definitions

So now that we know how the system finds effects for various surface type collisions, how do we find and create effects?

Effects are contained inside `Libs/MaterialEffects/FXLibs/` as pure XML files. For example, the definition of the previously used **collision:vegetation_spruce** effect is contained in `Libs/MaterialEffects/FXLibs/Collision.xml` with the following contents:

```
<FXLib>
  <Effect name="vegetation_spruce">
    <Particle>
      <Name>Snow.Vegetation.SpruceNeedleGroup</Name>
    </Particle>
  </Effect>
</FXLib>
```

This tells the engine to play the specified particle when the effect is triggered. For example, as we defined previously, if a material with the surface type of **mat_flesh** collides with another of the type **mat_vegetation**, the engine will spawn the `Snow.Vegetation.SpruceNeedleGroup` effect at the position of impact.

But what about sounds? Sounds can be played back via events in a similar fashion to particles; simply replace the `Particle` tag with `Sound` and specify the name of your sound as shown in the following code:

```
<Sound>
  <Name>Sounds/Animals:Animals:Pig</Name>
</Sound>
```

Now when the effect is played, we should be able to hear a pig squirm. That's what happens when you collide into vegetation, right?

> It's worth remembering that an effect does not have to contain one specific type of effect, but can also play multiple effects simultaneously. For example, based on the previous code, we could create a new effect that plays a sound and also spawns a particle effect when triggered.

Triggering custom events

It is also possible to trigger custom material effects, which is useful when, for example, creating footstep effects that should differ based on the interaction name.

	1	2	3
		mat_metal	mat_metal_nofric
	bullet	bulletimpacts:hit_mat_metal	bulletimpacts:hit_mat_metal
	tank125	bulletimpacts:grenade_hit_mat_default	bulletimpacts:grenade_hit_mat_default
	rocket	bulletimpacts:grenade_hit_mat_default	bulletimpacts:grenade_hit_mat_default
	MGbullet	bulletimpacts:hit_mat_metal	bulletimpacts:hit_mat_metal
	melee	bulletimpacts:melee_hit_mat_metal	bulletimpacts:melee_hit_mat_metal
	tornado	tornado:generic	tornado:generic
	explosivegrenade	collisions:grenade_default	collisions:grenade_default
	explosivegrenade_explode	bulletimpacts:grenade_hit_mat_default	bulletimpacts:grenade_hit_mat_default
	explosivegrenade_explode_underwater	bulletimpacts:grenade_hit_mat_water	bulletimpacts:grenade_hit_mat_water
	footstep_player	footstep_player:metal_thick	footstep_player:metal_thick
	footstep_grunt	footstep_grunt:metal_thick	footstep_grunt:metal_thick
	footstep	footstep_grunt:metal_thick	footstep_grunt:metal_thick
	bodyfall	foley:bf_metal_thick	foley:bf_metal_thick

> The colon (':') stands for the effect category, which is the name of the effect library we created in the `Libs/MaterialEffects/FXLibs/` folder.

The previous screenshot is a smaller selection of custom material effects that are triggered programmatically.

To obtain the ID of an effect, call `IMaterialEffects::GetEffectId`, by supplying the interaction name and the relevant surface type as shown in the following code.

```
IMaterialEffects *pMaterialEffects = gEnv->pGame-
  >GetIGameFramework()->GetIMaterialEffects();

TMFXEffectId effectId = pMaterialEffects-
  >GetEffectId("footstep_player", surfaceId);
```

There are many ways of obtaining surface identifiers. For example, casting a ray using `RayWorldIntersection` will allow us to get the collided surface ID via the `ray_hit::surface_idx` variable. We could also simply call `IMaterial::GetSurfaceTypeId` on any material instance.

We should now have the identifier of the `footstep_player` effect, based on the surface type we passed to `GetEffectId`. For example, by cross-referencing with the previous screenshot, and assuming that we passed the `mat_metal` identifier, we should have the ID of the `footstep_player:metal_thick` effect.

We can then execute the effect by calling `IMaterialEffects::ExecuteEffect` as shown:

```
SMFXRunTimeEffectParams params;
params.pos = Vec3(0, 0, 10);

bool result = gEnv->pGame->GetIGameFramework()-
  >GetIMaterialEffects()->ExecuteEffect(effectId, params);
```

It is also possible to get the effect resources by calling `IMaterialEffects::GetResources` as shown:

```
if(effectId != InvalidEffectId)
{
  SMFXResourceListPtr->pList = pMaterialEffects-
    >GetResources(effectId);

  if(pList && pList->m_particleList)
  {
    const char *particleEffectName = pList->m_particleList-
      >m_particleParams.name;
  }
}
```

Animation-based events and effects

Animation-based events can be used to trigger specific effects during a set time of an animation. For example, we could use this to link sounds to animations to make sure that the sound is always played in sync with its corresponding animation.

To start, open the **Character Editor** via the **Sandbox Editor**, load any character definition, and then select any animation.

Select the **Animation Control** tab at the bottom center of the window, and choose any time during the animation during which you want to play your sound.

When you have the slider positioned on the time your sound should be played at, click on **New Event**.

The **Name** field of the event should be **sound**, and set the **Parameter** field to the path of the sound that you want to play.

After clicking on **Save**, the sound should start playing along with the animation at the time specified.

Spawning particle emitters

As mentioned in the *Particle effects* section, particle effects are represented by the `IParticleEffect` interface. However, a particle effect is not the same as a particle emitter. The effect interface handles the properties of the default effect, and can spawn individual emitters that show the visual effect in the game.

Emitters are represented by the `IParticleEmitter` interface, and are most commonly retrieved by calling `IParticleEffect::Spawn`.

Exporting sounds by using FMod

So you want to export a few sounds to the engine? The first thing we need to do is create a new FMod project, via the **FMOD Designer**. To do so, start by opening the designer via `<Engine Root>/Tools/FmodDesigner/fmod_designer.exe`.

To create a new project, click on the **File** menu, select **New Project**, and then save the project to the location you see fit. We'll be saving ours to `Game/Sounds/Animals/ Animals.fdp`.

> For a more in-depth tutorial on the FMOD sound system, see the CryENGINE documentation at `http://docs.cryengine. com/display/SDKDOC3/The+FMOD+Designer`.

Adding sounds to the project

Now that we have a sound project, it's time to add a few sounds. To do so, make sure that you're in the **Events** menu, with the **Groups** tab activated as shown in the following screenshot:

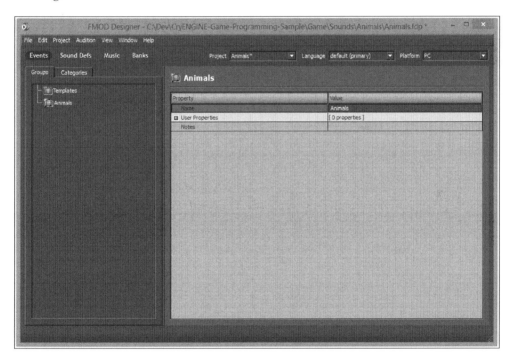

Now, to add a sound, simply drag a .wav file into the group you selected, and it should appear there. You can now navigate to **Project | Build**, or press *Ctrl + B*, in order to build the wave bank for your project, which is what the engine will load to detect the sounds.

By adding more sounds to the event group, the system will randomly pick a sound when the group is requested.

By selecting an event group in FMOD, we'll also be able to modify its properties, essentially tweaking how the sound is played when it is played back.

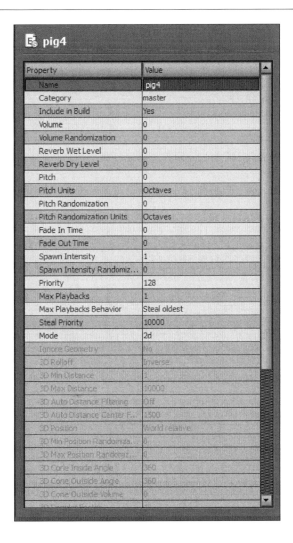

Property	Value
Name	pig4
Category	master
Include in Build	Yes
Volume	0
Volume Randomization	0
Reverb Wet Level	0
Reverb Dry Level	0
Pitch	0
Pitch Units	Octaves
Pitch Randomization	0
Pitch Randomization Units	Octaves
Fade In Time	0
Fade Out Time	0
Spawn Intensity	1
Spawn Intensity Randomiz...	0
Priority	128
Max Playbacks	1
Max Playbacks Behavior	Steal oldest
Steal Priority	10000
Mode	2d
Ignore Geometry	No
3D Rolloff	Inverse
3D Min Distance	1
3D Max Distance	10000
3D Auto Distance Filtering	Off
3D Auto Distance Center F...	1500
3D Position	World relative
3D Min Position Randomiza...	0
3D Max Position Randomiz...	0
3D Cone Inside Angle	360
3D Cone Outside Angle	360
3D Cone Outside Volume	0

Most properties statically affect the sound, whereas ending with **Randomization** creates an effect that is randomly applied at runtime. For example, by tweaking **Pitch Randomization**, we can ensure that the pitch of the sound will be randomly offset by the value we choose, giving the sound a unique touch.

Playing sounds

When playing audio, we have to differentiate between dynamic sounds triggered by the programmer, and static sounds that are triggered by the level creator.

There are multiple ways of triggering audio events, which should be evaluated based on the purpose of the sound.

Using SoundSpots

The soundspot entity exists to allow level designers to easily place an entity that will play a predefined sound in a specific area. The sound entity supports looping sounds, or playing them once each time it is triggered from a scripted event.

To use a soundspot, start by placing a new instance of the **SoundSpot** entity via the Rollupbar, or navigate to **Sound | Soundspot**. Once placed, you should see something similar to the example shown in following screenshot:

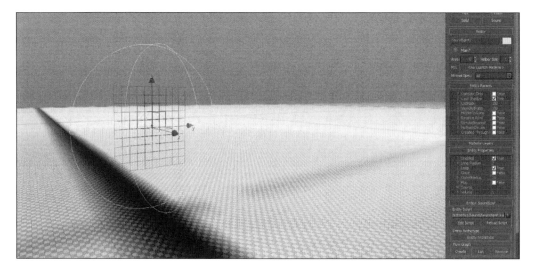

We can now assign a sound that should be played within the spot. To do so, click on the **Source** entity property and then choose a sound via the **Sound Browser** window as shown in the following screenshot:

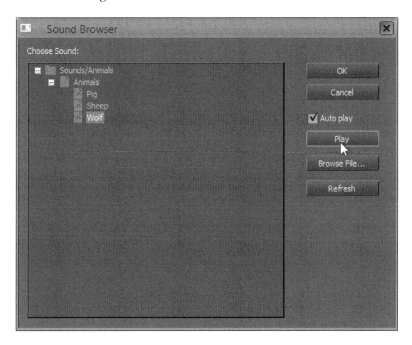

You can then set up **SoundSpot** to either always play the sound, or be triggered via flowgraph. For example, in the following screenshot, the soundspot will play its sound when the player uses the *K* key.

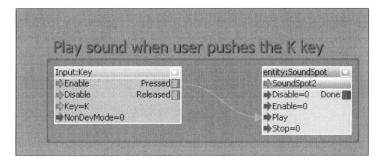

Programmatically playing sound

To programmatically play a sound, we'll first need to retrieve an `ISound` pointer relevant to the specific sound we're interested in playing, via `ISoundSystem::CreateSound` as shown:

```
ISound *pSound = gEnv->pSoundSystem-
  >CreateSound("Sounds/Animals:Animals:Pig", 0);
```

We can then play the sound directly via `ISound::Play`, or attach it to an entity's sound proxy:

```
IEntitySoundProxy *pSoundProxy = (IEntitySoundProxy *)pEntity-
  >CreateProxy(ENTITY_PROXY_SOUND);

if(pSoundProxy)
  pSoundProxy->PlySound(pSound);
```

By using an entity sound proxy, we can make sure that the sound follows that entity as it moves around the game world.

Sound flags

When creating sounds by using the `ISoundSystem::CreateSound interface`, we have the option to specify a set of flags that will affect the playback of our sound.

Some flags need to be set up in FMOD before they can be used. For example, sounds with 3D space effects have to be set up in FMOD before they can be used in the engine.

These flags are contained in `ISound.h` as preprocessor macros with the `FLAG_SOUND_` prefix. For example, we could apply the `FLAG_SOUND_DOPPLER` flag to our sound in order to have a Doppler effect simulated on playback.

Sound semantics

Semantics are essentially modifiers applied to sounds, and are required for each sound in order to have it played.

The different sound semantics can be viewed in `ISound.h` (in the CryCommon project), within the `ESoundSemantic` enum.

Summary

In this chapter, we have exported sounds from FMOD into the engine, and learned how to tweak them.

You should now know how to trigger sounds both via the Sandbox Editor and programmatically, and also have a working knowledge of material effects.

If you're not quite ready to move on to the next chapter, why not try expanding your knowledge? A possibility could be to dive into the particle editor and create your own particle, complete with custom effects and sounds.

In the next chapter, we'll be covering the process of debugging and profiling your game logic, aiding you in working more efficiently.

12
Debugging and Profiling

Creating efficient and bug-free code can be difficult. Therefore, the engine exposes a number of tools to help developers in this regard, allowing easy identification of bugs and visualization of performance problems.

It is important to keep the debugging and profiling tools in mind at all times when writing both game and engine logic, in order to make sure that your code runs optimally and can be easily scanned for issues. Simply adding a few game log warnings can be vital for saving a bunch of time when resolving future issues!

In this chapter we will cover the following topics:

- Learning common ways of debugging CryENGINE applications
- Utilizing the built-in profilers
- Creating our own console variables and commands

Debugging the game logic

Keeping your code bug-free can be very difficult, especially if you only rely on your debugger. CryENGINE exposes a number of systems for aiding the debugging of your code, even when you're not attached to the running process.

Always keep in mind which configuration you build the GameDll with. This can be changed before building your project in Visual Studio, as shown in the following screenshot:

By default, there are three primary configurations as shown in the following table:

Configuration name	Description
Profile	Used when developing the application, makes sure debug databases are generated.
Debug	Used when you need compilation optimizations turned off, as well as extra CryENGINE helpers that are turned on specifically for this mode.
Release	This mode is meant to be used earlier for final builds that are sent to end users.
	This configuration does a bunch of things, including disabling the generation of debug databases and multiple debug-only CryENGINE systems.
	It is also common practice for CryENGINE games to link all libraries such as CryGame into one Launcher application for security.

Logging to the console and files

The logging system allows for printing text to console and the `.log` file contained in the root file structure. The name of the log depends on which application was launched:

Log name	Description
`Game.log`	Used by the Launcher application.
`Editor.log`	Only used by the Sandbox Editor application.
`Server.log`	Used for the dedicated server.

Logging functionality is commonly used for very severe issues, or to warn designers of unsupported behavior.

The biggest benefit of logging severe errors and initialization statistics is that you'll often be able to figure out why your code is not working as it should on the end user's computer by simply reading their game log.

Log verbosity

The log verbosity is set by using the `log_verbosity` console variable (for the visual part of the console) and `log_writeToFileVerbosity` (for the log written to disk).

Verbosity determines which messages should be logged/displayed, and is useful for filtering out less severe messages.

Verbosity level	Description
-1 (no logging)	Suppresses all logged information, including `CryLogAlways`.
0 (always)	Suppresses all logged information, excluding that logged using `CryLogAlways`.
1 (error)	Same as level 0, but with additional errors.
2 (warning)	Same as level 1, but with additional warnings.
3 (message)	Same as level 2, but with additional messages.
4 (comment)	Highest verbosity, logs everything mentioned previously as well as additional comments.

Global log functions

The following is a list of global log functions:

- `CryLog`: This function logs a message to the console and file log, assuming log verbosity is 3 or higher.

  ```
  CryLog("MyMessage");
  ```

- `CryLogAlways`: This function logs a message to the console and file, assuming log verbosity is 0 or higher.

  ```
  CryLogAlways("This is always logged, unless log_verbosity
    is set to -1");
  ```

- `CryWarning`: This function outputs a warning to the log and console, prefixed by [Warning]. It is also useful for warning designers that they're using functionality incorrectly. It will only log to file if log verbosity is 2 or higher.

  ```
  CryWarning(VALIDATOR_MODULE_GAME, VALIDATOR_WARNING, "My
    warning!");
  ```

- `CryFatalError`: This function is used to designate that a severe error has occurred, and results in a message box followed by program termination.

  ```
  CryFatalError("Fatal error, shutting down!");
  ```

- `CryComment`: This function outputs a comment, assuming log verbosity is 4.

  ```
  CryComment("My note");
  ```

Note: Logging in C# is done by using the static `Debug` class. For example, to log a message, one would use `Debug.Log("message");`

To log using Lua, use the `System.Log` function, for example, `System.Log("MyMessage");`

The persistent debug

The persistent debug system allows the drawing of persistent helpers that give visual feedback on game logic. For example, the system is used in the following screenshot to draw the direction the player is facing at their world position on every frame, where each arrow lasts for a specified number of seconds before disappearing.

The system can bring very interesting effects, such as a way to see player rotation and physical interactions, as displayed in the free-to-play game SNOW:

C++

The `IPersistantDebug` interface can be accessed via the game framework as shown:

```
IPersistantDebug *pPersistantDebug = gEnv->pGame-
  >GetIGameFramework()->GetIPersistantDebug();
```

Prior to calling the various drawing functions, we'll need to call `IPersistantDebug::Begin` to signal that a new group of persistant debug should begin.

```
pPersistantDebug->Begin("myPersistentDebug", false);
```

The last boolean parameter specifies whether or not the system should clear all previously drawn persistent debug objects for the selected scope (`"myPersistentDebug"`).

We can now use the various **Add*** functions, such as `AddSphere`:

```
pPersistantDebug->AddSphere(Vec3(0, 0, 10), 0.3f, ColorF(1, 0, 0),
    2.0f);
```

In the previous snippet, the system will draw a red sphere of radius `0.3` at `0, 0, 10` in the game world. The sphere will disappear after `2` seconds.

C#

In C#, the persistent debug interface can be accessed by using the static `Debug` class. For example, to add a sphere as we did previously, use the following code:

```
Debug.DrawSphere(new Vec3(0, 0, 10), 0.3f, Color.Red, 2.0f);
```

CryAssert

The CryAssert system allows developers to make sure that certain variables are kept within boundaries. By doing checks that are only compiled in developer builds, it's possible to continuously test how systems interact with others. This is good for both performance and for making sure that your features are less bug-prone.

The system can be toggled by using the `sys_asserts` CVar, and may require defining the `USE_CRYASSERT` macro in your `StdAfx` header.

To do an assertion, use the `CRY_ASSERT` macro as shown:

```
CRY_ASSERT(pPointer != nullptr)
```

This will then be checked each time the code is run, except in release mode, and will output a big warning message box when the condition is false.

Profiling

When working with real-time products such as CryENGINE, programmers constantly have to consider the performance of their code. To aid in this, we'll be able to use the `profile` console variable.

The CVar allows for getting visual statistics on the most intensive parts of your code as shown in the following screenshot:

In the previous screenshot, profile was set to 1, the default mode, which sorts the most intensive functions being called for each frame.

Profile usages

Currently, the profile variable supports 13 different states as listed in the following table:

Value	Description
0	Default value; when this is set, the profiling system will be inactive.
1	Self time
2	Hierarchical time
3	Extended self time
4	Extended hierarchical time
5	Peaks time
6	Subsystem info
7	Calls number
8	Standard deviation
9	Memory allocation
10	Memory allocation (in bytes)
11	Stalls
-1	Used to enable the profiling system, without drawing information to the screen.

Profiling in C++

To profile in C++, we can make use of the FUNCTION_PROFILER pre-processor macro definition, as follows:

```
FUNCTION_PROFILER(GetISystem(), PROFILE_GAME);
```

The macro will set up the necessary profiler objects: one static CFrameProfiler object that is kept for the method, and one CFrameProfilerSection object that is created each time the method is run (and destroyed when returning).

If the profiler detects that your code runs heavily in relation to other engine functions, it will be displayed further up the profile graphs, as shown in the following screenshot:

If you want to debug a certain section of your code, you can also use the FRAME_PROFILER macro, which works the same as FUNCTION_PROFILER, except that it allows you to specify the name of the profiled section.

An example use case for FRAME_PROFILER is inside an `if` block, as the frame profiler section will be destroyed after the block is done:

```
if (true)
{
  FRAME_PROFILER("MyCheck", gEnv->pSystem, PROFILE_GAME);

  auto myCharArray = new char[100000];
  for(int i = 0; i < 100000; i++)
    myCharArray[i] = 'T';

  // Frame profiler section is now destroyed
}
```

We can now profile the previous code in the game, as shown in the following screenshot:

```
       Profile Mode: Self Time
       FrameTime: 0.48ms, OverheadTime: 0.02ms, LostTime: -0.02ms, PF/Sec: 11500
Count/ Time    Function

       0.14  CRenderer::RT_FlushTextMessages
       0.07  CD3D9Renderer::RT_EndFrame
       0.06  MyCheck
       0.05  CFrameProfileSystem::EndFrame
       0.05  CSystem::RenderEnd
       0.02  CFrameProfileSystem::Render
       0.01  Lua GC
    2/0.01  CBaseInput::PostInputEvent
```

Profiling in C#

It's also possible to profile your C# code in roughly the same manner. The difference is that we can't rely on destructors/finalizers in managed code, and will, therefore, have to do a bit of work ourselves.

The first thing we have to do is create a `CryEngine.Profiling.FrameProfiler` object which will persist for the lifetime of our entity. Then simply call `FrameProfiler.CreateSection` on the new frame profiler object each time you need to profile your function, and then call `FrameProfilerSection.End` on the resulting object when you're done using the following code:

```csharp
using CryEngine.Profiling;

public SpawnPoint()
{
  ReceiveUpdates = true;

  m_frameProfiler = FrameProfiler.Create("SpawnPoint.OnUpdate");
}

public override void OnUpdate()
{
  var section = m_frameProfiler.CreateSection();

  var stringArray = new string[10000];
  for(int i = 0; i < 10000; i++)
    stringArray[i] = "is it just me or is it laggy in here";
```

```
    section.End();
}


    FrameProfiler m_frameProfiler;
```

This will then result in the profiler listing `SpawnPoint.OnUpdate`, as shown in the following screenshot:

```
        Profile Mode: Self Time
        FrameTime: 0.44ms, OverheadTime: 0.02ms, LostTime: -0.01ms, PF/Sec: 2
Count/ Time    Function

    0.12  CRenderer::RT_FlushTextMessages
    0.07  CD3D9Renderer::RT_EndFrame
    0.06  SpawnPoint.OnUpdate
    0.05  CFrameProfileSystem::EndFrame
    0.03  CSystem::RenderEnd
    0.02  CFrameProfileSystem::Render
```

The console

Although not directly linked to debugging, the CryENGINE console provides the means for creating commands that can execute functions directly from the game, and the creation of variables that can be modified to change the way the world behaves.

> Fun fact: by using the hashtag (#) sign in the console, we can execute Lua directly in-game, for example, #System.Log("My message!");

Console variables

Console variables, commonly referred to as **CVars**, allow the exposure of variables in your code to the CryENGINE console, effectively allowing the tweaking of settings at runtime or through config (.cfg) files.

Pretty much every subsystem uses console variables at runtime in order to tweak the behaviour of systems without requiring code modifications.

Registering a CVar

When registering a new CVar, it's important to distinguish between by-reference variables and wrapped variables.

The difference is that a by-reference CVar points to a variable defined in your own code that updated directly when the value is changed via the console.

Wrapped variables contain the variable itself inside a specialized **ICVar** (C++) implementation inside `CrySystem.dll`.

By-reference, CVars are most commonly used, as they do not require calling `IConsole::GetCVar` every time we want to know the value of the console variable.

In C++

To register a by-reference console variable in C++, call `IConsole::Register` as shown:

```
gEnv->pConsole->Register("g_myVariable", &m_myVariable, 3.0f,
    VF_CHEAT, "My variable description!");
```

Now, the default value of the `g_myVariable` CVar will be `3.0f`. If we changed the value via the console, `m_myVariable` will be updated immediately.

> To find out what the `VF_CHEAT` flag does, see the *Flags* section discussed further.

To register a wrapped console variable, use `IConsole::RegisterString`, `RegisterFloat`, or `RegisterInt`.

In C#

To register a by-reference console variable via CryMono, use `CVar.RegisterFloat` or `CVar.RegisterInt`, as shown in the following code:

```
float m_myVariable;

CVar.RegisterFloat("g_myCSharpCVar", ref m_myVariable, "My
    variable is awesome");
```

> Due to the backend structure of C++ and C# strings being different, creating by-reference string CVars is not possible.

If you prefer to use wrapped variables, use `CVar.Register`.

Flags

When registering a new CVar, the developer should specify a default flag. The flags control how the variable behaves when modified or queried.

- VF_NULL: This flag is set to zero, and is used when no other flags are present.
- VF_CHEAT: This flag is used to prevent changes to the variable when cheats are enabled, for example, in release mode or multiplayer.
- VF_READONLY: This flag can never be changed by the user.
- VF_REQUIRE_LEVEL_RELOAD: This flag warns the user that a change to the variable will require a level reload to come into effect.
- VF_REQUIRE_APP_RESTART: This flag warns the user that a change will require an application restart to come into effect.
- VF_MODIFIED: This flag is set when the variable is modified.
- VF_WASINCONFIG: This flag is set if the variable is changed via a configuration (.cfg) file.
- VF_RESTRICTEDMODE: This flag is set if the variable should be visible and usable in restricted (release) console mode.
- VF_INVISIBLE: This flag is set if the variable should not be visible to the user in the console.
- VF_ALWAYSONCHANGE: This flag always accepts the new value, and calls on-change callbacks even if the value stayed the same.
- VF_BLOCKFRAME: This flag blocks the execution of further console commands for one frame after the variable was used.
- VF_CONST_CVAR: This flag is set if the variable should not be editable via configuration (.cfg) files.
- VF_CHEAT_ALWAYS_CHECK: This flag is set if the variable is very vulnerable, and should be checked continuously.
- VF_CHEAT_NOCHECK: This flag is same as VF_CHEAT, except that it will not be checked due to changes to it being harmless.

Console variable groups

In order to facilitate the creation of different system specifications (Low / Medium / High / Very High graphic levels), otherwise called **Sys Spec**, we can utilize CVar groups. These groups allow the value of multiple CVars to be changed simultaneously whenever the spec is changed.

If you are unsure of what Sys Specs do, read the *System specifications* section discussed later in this chapter.

To change the system spec, the user can simply change the value of the `sys_spec` console variable. Once changed, the engine will parse the linked spec file in `Engine/Config/CVarGroups/` and set the CVar values defined.

For example, if the `sys_spec_GameEffects` CVar is changed, the engine will open `Engine/Config/CVarGroups/sys_spec_GameEffects.cfg`.

The `sys_spec_Full` group is considered the root group, and is what is triggered when the `sys_spec` CVar is changed. It is set to update all subgroups, such as `sys_spec_Quality`, when it is changed.

Cfg structure

The structure of a CVar group configuration file is relatively easy to understand. As an example, see the following `sys_spec_GameEffects` file:

```
[default]
; default of this CVarGroup
= 3

i_lighteffects = 1
g_ragdollUnseenTime = 2
g_ragdollMinTime = 13
g_ragdollDistance = 30

[1]
g_ragdollMinTime = 5
g_ragdollDistance = 10

[2]
g_ragdollMinTime = 8
g_ragdollDistance = 20

[3]

[4]
g_ragdollMinTime = 15
g_ragdollDistance = 40
```

The first three lines defines which spec is default for this configuration file, in this case High (3).

Following the default spec are the default values for CVars in the high spec. These will be used as a baseline and applied to all specs, unless overridden.

Postioned after the default spec are Low Spec (`[1]`), Medium Spec (`[2]`) and Very High Spec (`[4]`). The CVars placed after the definitions define what values the variables should be set to in that spec.

System specifications

The current system spec is determined by the value of the `sys_spec` CVar. Changing the value of the variable will automatically load shaders and CVar groups that have been tweaked specifically for that spec. For example, if the game is running a bit badly on your PC, you might want to change the spec to Low (1).

- 0: Custom
- 1: Low
- 2: Medium
- 3: High
- 4: Very High
- 5: Xbox 360
- 6: PlayStation 3

Console commands

Console commands (commonly referred to as **CCommands**), are essentially functions that have been mapped to console variables. However, instead of changing the value of a referenced variable when the command is entered into the console, the call will trigger a function that was specified while registering the command.

Note that console variables can also specify `On Change` callbacks that are automatically invoked when the value is changed. Prefer console commands when an internal variable is not relevant to your intent.

Registering a console command in C#

To register a console command in C#, use `ConsoleCommand.Register` as shown in the following code:

```
public void OnMyCSharpCommand(ConsoleCommandArgs e)
{
}


ConsoleCommand.Register("MyCSharpCommand", OnMyCSharpCommand, "C#
  CCommands are awesome.");
```

Triggering `MyCSharpCommand` in the console will now result in the `OnMyCSharpCommand` function being invoked.

Arguments

When your callback is triggered, you'll be able to retrieve the set of arguments that were added after the command itself. For example, if the user were to activate the command by typing `MyCommand 2`, we might want to retrieve the `2` part of the string.

To do so, use the `ConsoleCommandArgs.Args` array, and specify which index the argument you want is at. For the previous example, it would look like the following code:

```
string firstArgument = null;
if(e.Args.Length >= 1)
  firstArgument = e.Args[0];
```

 To retrieve the full command line that was specified with the command, use `ConsoleCommandArgs.FullCommandLine`.

Creating a Console Command in C++

To add a new console command in C++, use `IConsole::AddCommand` as shown:

```
void MyCommandCallback(IConsoleCmdArgs *pCmdArgs)
{
}
gEnv->pConsole->AddCommand("MyCommand", MyCommandCallback,
  VF_NULL, "My command is great!");
```

After compiling and starting the engine, you will be able to type `MyCommand` in the console and trigger your `MyCommandCallback` function.

Summary

In this chapter, we have:

- Learned how to use a selection of the engine's debugging tools
- Profiled our code to ensure optimal performance
- Learned what console variables (CVars) are, and how to use them
- Created custom console commands

You should now have a basic understanding of how to best program in CryENGINE. Make sure that you always keep profiling and debugging methods in mind, in order to ensure that your code runs optimally.

Assuming that you've read the book's chapters in order, you should now be aware of the workings of the most important engine systems. We hope you enjoyed the read, and wish you the best of luck with using your newly-gained CryENGINE knowledge!

Index

G

Game folder 20
game logic
  debugging 227
game logic, debugging
  Profile configuration 228
  Release configuration 228
game mode
  about 72
  registering 72, 73
game object extension
  about 67
  activating 69
  creating, in C++ 67-69
game objects
  about 67
  used, for networking 163
  extensions 67
game rules
  about 71
  IGameRules interface 72
  level, loading 73
game rules interface
  custom game modes, creating 75
  game object extension, registering 74
  implementing 73, 74
GetConfiguration
  Flownode configuration flags 47
  implementing 45, 46
  node configuration, assigning to 47
  ports, creating 46, 47
  ProcessEvent, implementing 48, 49
GetDefaultProperty 62
GetEditorClassInfo() method 60
GetName() method 60
GetPort: functions 48
GetProperty 62
GetPropertyCount 62
GetPropertyInfo 62
GetTexture2D function 197, 200
global log functions
  CryComment 229
  CryFatalError 229
  CryLog 229
  CryLogAlways 229
  CryWarning 229

goal pipes, AI
  about 120
  custom pipes, creating 121
  selecting 121
graph 26
graph entity 28

H

hardware mouse
  implementing 101
Headquarters
  end game event, adding 84
  implementing 84
Headquarters entity
  creating 84, 85
Heads-Up Display (HUD) 152
helper types
  b 177
  c 177
  f(#) 177
  g 177
  j 177
  l 177
  t(#) 177
HUD:DisplayDebugMessage node 34
humanName parameter 46
HWND 193

I

I3DEngine::RenderWorld
  about 192
  I3DEngine::RenderWorld flags 196
  using 194, 195
I3DEngine::RenderWorld flags
  about 196
  SHDF_ALLOW_AO 196
  SHDF_ALLOWHDR 196
  SHDF_ALLOWPOSTPROCESS 196
  SHDF_ALLOW_WATER 196
  SHDF_DO_NOT_CLEAR_Z_BUFFER 196
  SHDF_NOASYNC 196
  SHDF_NO_DRAWCAUSTICS 196
  SHDF_NO_DRAWNEAR 196
  SHDF_STREAM_SYNC 196
  SHDF_ZPASS_ONLY 196
IActionControlle::Queue function 114

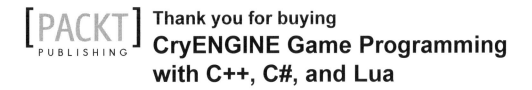

Thank you for buying
CryENGINE Game Programming with C++, C#, and Lua

About Packt Publishing

Packt, pronounced 'packed', published its first book "*Mastering phpMyAdmin for Effective MySQL Management*" in April 2004 and subsequently continued to specialize in publishing highly focused books on specific technologies and solutions.

Our books and publications share the experiences of your fellow IT professionals in adapting and customizing today's systems, applications, and frameworks. Our solution based books give you the knowledge and power to customize the software and technologies you're using to get the job done. Packt books are more specific and less general than the IT books you have seen in the past. Our unique business model allows us to bring you more focused information, giving you more of what you need to know, and less of what you don't.

Packt is a modern, yet unique publishing company, which focuses on producing quality, cutting-edge books for communities of developers, administrators, and newbies alike. For more information, please visit our website: www.packtpub.com.

Writing for Packt

We welcome all inquiries from people who are interested in authoring. Book proposals should be sent to author@packtpub.com. If your book idea is still at an early stage and you would like to discuss it first before writing a formal book proposal, contact us; one of our commissioning editors will get in touch with you.

We're not just looking for published authors; if you have strong technical skills but no writing experience, our experienced editors can help you develop a writing career, or simply get some additional reward for your expertise.

CryENGINE 3 Game Development: Beginner's Guide

ISBN: 978-1-84969-200-7   Paperback: 354 pages

Discover how to use the CryENGINE 3 free SDK, the next-generation, real-time game development tool

1. Begin developing your own games of any scale by learning to harness the power of the Award Winning CryENGINE® 3 game engine

2. Build your game worlds in real-time with CryENGINE® 3 Sandbox as we share insights into some of the tools and features useable right out of the box.

3. Harness your imagination by learning how to create customized content for use within your own custom games through the detailed asset creation examples within the book.

CryENGINE 3 Cookbook

ISBN: 978-1-84969-106-2   Paperback: 324 pages

Over 90 recipes written by Crytek developers for creating third-generation real-time games

1. Begin developing your AAA game or simulation by harnessing the power of the award winning CryENGINE3

2. Create entire game worlds using the powerful CryENGINE 3 Sandbox.

3. Create your very own customized content for use within the CryENGINE3 with the multiple creation recipes in this book

Please check **www.PacktPub.com** for information on our titles

Torque 3D Game Development Cookbook

ISBN: 978-1-84969-354-7   Paperback: 380 pages

Over 80 pratical recipes and hidden game for getiing the most out of the Torque 3D game engine

1. Clear step-by-step instruction and practical examples to advance your understanding of Torque 3D and all of its sub-systems

2. Explore essential topics such as graphics, sound, networking and user input

3. Helpful tips and techniques to increase the potential of your Torque 3D games

Cocos2d for iPhone 1 Game Development Cookbook

ISBN: 978-1-84951-400-2   Paperback: 446 pages

Over 90 recipes for iOS 2D game development using cocos2d

1. Discover advanced Cocos2d, OpenGL ES, and iOS techniques spanning all areas of the game development process

2. Learn how to create top-down isometric games, side-scrolling platformers, and games with realistic lighting

3. Full of fun and engaging recipes with modular libraries that can be plugged into your project

Please check **www.PacktPub.com** for information on our titles

Made in the USA
San Bernardino, CA
08 December 2013